WALK IN THIS LIGHT

WALK IN THIS LIGHT

*Living out our baptism and
confirmation*

Richard Giles

CANTERBURY
PRESS
Norwich

© Richard Giles 2013

First published in 2013 by the Canterbury Press Norwich
Editorial office
3rd Floor, Invicta House, 108–114 Golden Lane,
London EC1Y 0TG

Canterbury Press is an imprint of Hymns Ancient &
Modern Ltd (a registered charity)
13A Hellesdon Park Road, Norwich,
Norfolk, NR6 5DR, UK

www.canterburypress.co.uk

Scripture quotations are from the New Revised Standard
Version of the Bible, copyright 1989 by the Division
of Christian Education of the National Council
of the Churches of Christ in the USA.
Used by permission. All rights reserved.

The Author has asserted his right under the Copyright,
Designs and Patents Act, 1988,
to be identified as the Author of this Work

British Library Cataloguing in Publication data

A catalogue record for this book is available
from the British Library

978 1 84825 327 8

Typeset by Manila Typesetting Company
Printed and bound by
Scandbook AB, Sweden

Contents

You have received the light
of Christ, walk in this light
all the days of your life.

'The Sending Out',
Common Worship: Christian Initiation

FOREWORD

'. . . you give your people new life in the water of baptism.'
Common Worship: Christian Initiation:
Holy Baptism, The Collect

We have been buried with him by baptism into death,
so that, just as Christ was raised from the dead by the glory
of the Father, so we too might walk in newness of life.
Romans 6:4

If you have turned this page because you are preparing for the rites of Christian Initiation, whether baptism or confirmation, you are in for the journey of your life. Forget backpacking round Tibet, or white-water rafting in the Rockies, this is the real adventure; to follow Jesus of Nazareth, unconditionally, until our dying day. Hold on tight!

Jesus taught us how to live and how to die, and how to let love – of the sacrificial, uncompromising, tough kind – be our primary guide and our only weapon in dealing with life in all its fullness, variety and occasional cruelty. By being transparent with the love of

God, Jesus taught us how to be fully human, to rise to our utmost potential, and to know joy beyond all imagining. He gives us what cannot be seized or stolen, and is ours for ever.[1]

Christian Initiation incorporates us into the body of men and women, across the world and down the ages, who have thrown in their lot with this wonderful, captivating, unpredictable, compelling Teacher. From now on you will in a deep sense belong to him, and thereby be able to live life to the uttermost. The American writer and illustrator Maurice Sendak[2] was described as someone who was 'fantastically, ebulliently alive',[3] and that's a pretty good description too of being gathered up into God's holy community of faith, living out the Way of Jesus the Christ.

The precise details of how best to make a new member of the Church varies from place to place and from tradition to tradition – hardly surprising, given the nature of human beings and the passing of 2,000 years.

Baptism is basically a ceremony of ritual washing and cleansing, known in pre-Christian times but given new depth of meaning by Jesus who promised that those who received this ritual in his name would be washed not just in water but in the Holy Spirit of God.

Other elements – of signing, anointing, the laying-on of hands, and being re-clothed – may or may not be added. Depending on which church community we find ourselves part of, Christian Initiation can sometimes be the bare essentials, sometimes the full works with bells and whistles. Whatever the details of the outward form, in baptism we submit ourselves afresh to God and, renouncing the past, give our lives over to Jesus as God's Chosen One.

When baptism occurs in infancy, we shall be eager later on, once we are old enough to make our own decisions, to reaffirm publicly in the rite of confirmation the promises earlier made on our behalf, and to claim for ourselves the gift of God's spirit.

The term 'baptismal life' will be used in this book to describe the life shared by all who have been admitted into the household of faith by baptism, at whatever age, who have publicly affirmed their faith as a believing adult, and who have committed themselves to a lifelong journey of faith. No matter by what route we travelled, here we are at last; part of the community of the baptized, the holy people of God, washed, re-clothed and marked with the sign of Christ.

The book attempts to set out a few navigational pointers for the journey of baptismal life – that is, the life lived by the community of the baptized, from the day of our Christian initiation to the day of our death. We learn to recognize signposts and heed warnings along the road, and to value the experience and insights of those who have travelled this way before us.

Once we know both our need of God and the wonder of God's mercy, our journey can begin. Once we have taken our first steps, we shall find to our surprise and delight that we are one of many, that we are joined by countless companions on the road, and that our learning to travel joyfully and thankfully together is at the heart of the Christian experience. This is our baptismal life, in which we are fantastically and ebulliently alive.

> We are pilgrims on a journey,
> fellow trav'llers on the road;
> we are here to help each other
> walk the mile and bear the load.[4]

Notes

1 John 16:22: 'and no one will take your joy away from you'.
2 Maurice Sendak, 1928–2012, writer and illustrator of children's literature, most notably *Where the Wild Things Are*.
3 Emma Brockes, *Guardian*, 8 May 2012.
4 Richard Gillard, 'Brother, sister, let me serve you', verse 2, *Scripture in Song*, 1977.

I

ON THE WAY

'. . . disciples with us on the Way of Christ.'
Common Worship: Christian Initiation: Call and Celebration

While they were talking and discussing,
Jesus himself came near and went with them.
Luke 24.15

In these words the Church community recognizes and honours those presenting themselves as candidates for Christian Initiation as new disciples eager to learn the Christian Way within the life of the people of God. The president (the priest or bishop leading worship) speaks of our 'joy and privilege' in welcoming these new brothers and sisters, for they are in themselves a 'sign of the journey of faith to which we are all called'.[1]

People of the Way was always how others described followers of Christ at first, and how they saw themselves.[2] It indicates a journey towards rather than a destination arrived at; a suggestion of how things *might* be, rather than a rigid sense of how they *must* be. The Way beckons us onwards, revealing broader vistas over each new rise.

As time passed and the desire for security and certainty prevailed, the Church came to look less like a Way and more like an institution. With official recognition of Christianity as the state religion in the fourth century, the Church gained strength and stability and a respite from persecution. But a vital spark was lost, as the desire to move and explore was gradually stifled by a preference for staying put.

The artist David Hockney said of creativity, 'if you're not moving, in a way you're dead,'[3] and that goes for us as we seek our own place on the way of Christ. If once we cease moving and exploring we will have lost our grasp on the full ebullient life that should be ours. We shall find that we no longer run to the top of the nearest hill to gaze with excitement at the new horizons beyond, content instead to linger in the valley.

As a child I used to love how Rupert Bear[4] would climb the highest tree he could find to gaze across the woodland stretching into the distance, on the lookout for smoke rising from a gypsy encampment perhaps, or anything different, anything new, which he and Bill Badger could explore. From my bedroom window on the edge of Birmingham I too gazed over the treetops towards the Forest of Arden, planning bike rides in the holidays. These expeditions would involve some degree of anxiety for a timid boy of 12 – punctures, dogs and menacing youths – but still the way beckoned, and each time I ventured a little further into the unknown.

On the move as God's people we discover not just new sights and new encounters, but our very identity.

The Israelites in their escape from slavery in Egypt discovered God on the way, moving before them as a cloud by day and a fire by night.[5] Only through undertaking that risky journey into the unknown did they encounter God on the road, the Ark symbolizing for them the presence of God who had pitched his tent alongside theirs, a nomad too.[6]

Jesus kept on the move throughout his ministry, teaching those who followed that 'the Son of Man has nowhere to lay his head'.[7] Animals have burrows and birds have nests, but he was of no fixed abode, accepting hospitality where it was given. This is a demanding road, and we can only travel along it because Jesus has gone ahead, marking the route for us. Like hill-walkers when the mist descends, we can look for, and find with enormous relief, the fresh imprint of a boot on the path we follow.

The journey of the baptismal life requires a proper map rather than satellite navigation. We are not free simply to punch in 'the kingdom of heaven' as our destination and wait to be told by a disembodied voice how to get there. We have to be fully engaged in mapping the route and finding the path. There is no automatic system to do it for us.

4

This requires orientating ourselves correctly (holding the map the right way up is a start) so that we head in the right direction, towards our destination, not away from it, or in circles. Rarely is our path a straight line, and we shall need to check frequently our navigation points – ranging from the scriptures, the tradition of the Church, to common sense – to make sure we are on the right track.

Sometimes the way shown on the map is found to be impassable on the ground, the path ahead closed off. At other times, a view opens up that reveals clearly a safe and secure way ahead, differing from the official route, enabling us to strike out on our own. Here we learn to trust our own judgement, folding up the map for a while. Good navigation involves the skill of reading the landscape and knowing when to change course, rather than clinging stubbornly to a path that peters out. Through honing our navigation skills we steadily gain confidence, maturing into responsible discipleship rather than regressing into childish dependency.

As people on the Way we likewise hone our skills in navigating our way through life. This we do through our daily prayer, our reading of the scriptures and our learning to be still. We have huge resources at our disposal, and the whole breadth and variety of Christian experience to draw on, through history and across the world. We can also cross-reference with other faith traditions as we move forward, for as the Buddhist monk Thich Nhat Hanh says, 'truth has no boundaries'.[8] The deepest truths are those common to all humanity, and checking our own insights with those of revered holy men and women who have trodden paths parallel to ours will serve to confirm, not compromise, all that is good and true in us and in our particular tradition.

Throughout our journeying we remind ourselves that we won't be doing this alone; in fact we aren't allowed to. This Christian journey is a group exercise, a shared venture. We may start out feeling solitary, but as we emerge from our own little doorway onto the street, we find ourselves caught up in a wonderful company of fellow travellers streaming along the road, a rag-tag collection of all sorts and sizes and colours of humanity, all heading the same way, glad of one another's company, and appreciative of the different gifts everyone brings to the party. Together we're ready for anything.

Once we have begun our journey, nothing will ever be quite the same again. We see things through different eyes, with more open hearts, with more forgiving grace, and with a growing sense of wonder. The poet William Blake[9] once said, 'I walked the other evening to the end of the earth, and touched the sky with my finger.'[10]

We too are enabled to do just that when we, the community of the baptized, assemble every Sunday, not just to talk, or listen or pray, but to touch holy things, and in so doing to realize that we ourselves are the holy, beloved, children of God, a little lower than the angels, crowned with glory and honour.[11] Yes, that really does refer to you and me, transformed by our life together in the assembly of faith.

'We declare to you', says the author of the first letter of John, 'what we have seen with our eyes, what we have looked at and touched with our hands.'[12] Ours is a tactile experience of God, earthed in the world around us, in which touch is more important than words, or ideas or professions of faith. To be alive is miracle enough, but to walk this road in such wonderful company and to see and to touch and to handle the things of God is truly wondrous.

In our journey as disciples of Jesus there will be moments of danger, fear or discouragement. We may turn aside for a moment, or even begin to turn back, but when we waver we remember that 'we are surrounded by so great a cloud of witnesses',[13] the glorious company who walk alongside us now, and those who have gone before.

Above all we look to the One who has trodden this path before us, blazing the trail, marking the way. Jesus has not sent us into the unknown, but onto a path he has pioneered for us, for he is the 'pioneer and perfecter of our faith'.[14] He taught us much by his words and deeds, but it was above all by his going the distance, to his own great cost, that he made everything possible for those who follow. This we now do with growing confidence and excitement:

> Thou carriest us, and Thou dost go before,
> Thou art the journey, and the journey's end.[15]

For the disciples of Jesus, our journey is not an optional extra for those who enjoy travel, or a once-in-a-lifetime pilgrimage to a holy place, but a movement inseparable from our identity. 'This journey is itself a process of discovery and transformation',[16] a process by which we appropriate 'patterns of belief, prayer and behaviour'[17] that give structure to our Christian life.

Journey may form part of our regular routine – to work, to school, to the shops – but when did we last make a *real* journey, a journey into the unknown? When did we last take a risk, cook without a recipe, go cross-country without a map? If we stop journeying, we lose touch with our deepest selves and forget who we are and how far we have travelled.

Journey defines us, it's what we do. We are men and women of the Way.

Notes

1 'Welcome of Disciples on the Way of Faith', *Common Worship: Christian Initiation*, London: Church House Publishing, 2005, p. 33.

2 Acts 19.9, 23; 22.4.

3 Martin Gayford, *A Bigger Message*, London: Thames and Hudson, 2011, p. 180.

4 Rupert Bear, the children's comic strip character, first appeared in the *Daily Express* in 1936 and still continues.

5 Exod. 40.38.

6 Lev. 26.11–12.

7 Luke 9.58.

8 Thich Nhat Hanh, *Living Buddha, Living Christ*, New York: Riverhead, 1995, p. 154.

9 William Blake, poet and mystic, 1757–1827.

10 Rachel Campbell-Johnston, *Mysterious Wisdom*, London: Bloomsbury, 2012, p. 75.

11 Ps. 8.5 and Heb. 2.7.

12 1 John 1.1.

13 Heb. 12.1.

14 Heb. 12.2.

15 Boethius (480–524), in prison awaiting execution, in Helen Waddell, tr., *More Latin Lyrics*, ed. Dame Felicitas Corrigan, London: Gollancz, 1976.

16 *Common Worship: Christian Initiation*, p. 8.

17 *Common Worship: Christian Initiation*, p. 10.

2

WASHED

'Here we are washed by the Holy Spirit and made clean.'
Common Worship:
Christian Initiation: Holy Baptism, Introduction

Simon Peter said to him,
'Lord, not my feet only, but also my hands and my head!'
John 13.9

Introducing the rite of baptism, the president of the liturgy summarizes what undergoing Christian Initiation will mean for the candidate, explaining that a primary theme of baptism is being washed clean by the Spirit of God.

Peeling an orange is an activity that makes me want to wash my hands afterwards. I have never got on well with oranges; the pith always gets rammed down my thumbnails and the juice goes everywhere. Oranges leave a distinctive smell, and they stick to you. No amount of licking of fingers ever seems to do the trick; nothing short of a rinse under the tap with warm soapy water will do.

Sometimes in our spiritual journey we find ourselves with a split orange in our hands, pith and juice and pips and all, something that makes us feel sticky and a little unclean, with a smell that lingers. In other words, we encounter sin, the stuff that 'clings so closely'[1] and that, as followers of Christ, we need to take seriously while not letting it overwhelm us.

The cry of outraged innocence, 'It wasn't me, miss, it was him!' is heard today not only in the classroom but the workplace, the law courts, and at press conferences

given by politicians or financiers exonerating themselves from blame.

Equally reprehensible, but at the other extreme, is
the culture in which everyone is guilty, all of the time.
This oppressive spiritual approach held sway in the
Church for much of Christian history, with Augustine
of Hippo[2] and the Reformer John Calvin[3] just two of
the big names who waded in to lay a heavy burden of
guilt and worthlessness upon humankind.

Somewhere between these two extremes of denying
responsibility or wallowing in guilt, the community
of the baptized creates a safe place where sin can be
recognized for what it is, dealt with calmly and realis-
tically, and put behind us. We recognize that accepting responsibility for wrongdoing is the first stage of
healing and growing into maturity. When the buck
stops with us, we know how to deal with it.

The experience of certain things that stick to us and
won't let go is all too familiar; an unkind word spoken in haste, a friend let down, a loved one betrayed,
or a failure to speak out, to act in time. In these things
we don't just break a rule, we fall short of what God
longs for us to be. Furthermore, we make ourselves

thoroughly miserable in the process. Remorse destroys peace of mind, and going over and over these events can cripple us. Through good habits of prayer and spiritual discipline we can go some way to restoring a proper balance, but usually it's not long before our need of good counsel and the reassurance of fellow pilgrims becomes clear.

For the older generation who grew up before the era of the daily shower, having a bath was a once-a-week ritual, amazing as that may sound today, and involved considerable pre-planning and much coaxing of boilers and immersion heaters. The holy assembly likewise has a weekly bath time, when every Sunday we gather at the baptismal water of the font to be spiritually washed and made clean so that, with renewed hearts and minds, we feel able once again to 'make Eucharist' (offer thanksgiving) to God.[4] Here we acknowledge our need of God's mercy, and our need to wash and be clean. God can then work with us and upon us, and we can begin again.

Significantly, when Peter preaches to the eager crowds at the beginning of the Christian story, there's more to it than just the washing. He urged repentance 'so that times of refreshing may come from the presence of the Lord'.[5] We are not just washed, we are refreshed, pampered and fussed over, emerging from the baptismal waters, scrubbed down, shiny new, and glowing all over.

The Church's Sacrament of Reconciliation deals with the serious stuff, and is an invaluable component of our spiritual check-up once or twice a year. The sacrament provides us with a beautiful and well-trodden path home to God whenever we are in need of a good scrub-down. The way back home can seem a hard road at the beginning, but is transformed into profound joy as we experience at the end of it God revealed to us as a loving Father, running towards the penitent with outstretched arms.[6]

Under 'M' in my battered commonplace book, begun in theological college days, whereas there are lots of entries for 'mission', and 'ministry' and 'mystery', there is only one for 'mercy'. Perhaps that goes to show the arrogance of the young, but in any event it is a winner.

The quotation is from a sermon from the great priest-poet John Donne, and it reminds us that: 'His mercy hath no relation to time, no limitation in time, it is not first, nor last, but eternal, everlasting.'[7] When we step out of our weekly bath as God's people, there is our loving mother the Church, wrapping us around in God's everlasting mercy. 'Their troubles, their joys, the best of them, the worst of them, went like homing pigeons to their mother.'[8]

Having come to God in true humility and in sorrow for our wrongdoing, we discover anew that we are held in love by the *mercy* of God. Then humankind comes of age, standing before God with heads erect and arms open, precisely because we know ourselves to be 'ransomed, healed, restored, forgiven'.[9]

At St Catherine's Sandal, Wakefield, a large cruciform baptismal pool is the first thing encountered on entering the worship space; it's so big that one almost falls over it. There is no chance of anyone missing it, nor should they.

Water has always been around at the entrance to church buildings to remind us who we are. A holy water stoup near the door, or the font filled with water, enables us to dip our finger in the water every time we enter the worship space, and to make on our forehead the same sign of the cross as was made for us in baptism. This little act of consecration begins our time of prayer, our sitting in silence, our pausing before the mystery. Such godly habits as a detour to a church building on our way to work or to the shops will punctuate our week with the presence of God. With great thankfulness we begin again, and again, as often and as frequently as we desire.

When we gather for our liturgical celebrations it is at the font that we deliberately get wet, enjoying the water, experiencing it in various ways as a sign of our new life. We have water thrown at us in the sprinkling, we touch it delightedly, we use it to mark one another's forehead with the sign of the cross, proclaiming that we are being washed and renewed, reconciled with God and with each other.

Our getting wet each Sunday is a symbol too of our immersion in the love and sheer goodwill of those around us in the assembly. Here are open smiles, direct gazes, and an evident readiness to give, to risk, to lay down our lives for one another. Whatever has happened to us in the week, here we are reawakened, here new life is breathed into us.

For us, the font takes the place of the fountain in the village square where the community gathers or just hangs out (well, they do in countries where it's hot enough). It is good when the font can always be kept brim-full of water (sometimes it awaits only a volunteer to offer to do this) or, as we begin to see more and more, when the old font can be made part of a real pool. We can usefully take a fresh look at our own worship space and observe how we make use of the font and whether a better connection might be made between what we say about the theory of baptism and what we actually do in worship. It may need just a sincere question from the new kid on the block to get the ball rolling.

The baptized community comes to the font thirsty for the water, finding to our delight that God does not measure it out carefully, or ration it sparingly. God does not deal in tiny trickles, or puddles, or damp sponges in holy water stoups, for 'the river of God is full of water'.[10] We are utterly drenched in the love of God, for 'deep calls to deep in the thunder of your waterfalls; all your breakers and waves have gone over me'.[11]

All we have to do is to so position ourselves under the shower of God's love, that every nook and cranny of us is made clean. No matter what has gone before, or how far we have marred the image of God within us, by God's grace we shall scrub up well.

But water is not always so benign, for it menaces as well as sparkles. Although irrigating and life-giving, rivers can also burst their banks, overwhelm and destroy.

Just a few inches of water are sufficient to drown us; it spells death as well as life. As a non-swimmer I have never overcome my fear of water, an element that for me remains totally alien. I panic when my feet cannot touch the bottom and this strange watery world threatens to engulf me. What others delight in, I dread.

It is entirely fitting, therefore, that water is the element used in the rite of baptism by which we pass through death into life. 'Do you not know', asks Paul, 'that all of us who have been baptized into Christ Jesus were baptized into his death?'[12] With Christ we enter into life through death.

Baptism doesn't come cheap, and it is right that we consider the cost. Are we ready to leap into the water, which is always colder, and more powerful than we imagine? Baptism requires us to die a little death, to submit, to submerge ourselves in something over which we have no control, to go beyond the point when our feet can touch the bottom.

But in so doing we are gathered up into life in all its glorious and triumphal fullness, that fantastic and ebullient life we spoke of earlier. We step boldly into the waters, knowing that Jesus passed this way before, and that in dying we shall discover how to live.

Washed by the Holy Spirit and made clean, we are embraced and lifted up out of the water by the wounded, risen Lord.

Notes

1 Heb. 12.1.
2 Augustine of Hippo, 354–430, a theologian who has dominated Christian thought for 1,500 years.
3 John Calvin, 1509–64.
4 The English word 'Eucharist' comes from the Greek *eucharistia* meaning 'thanksgiving'.
5 Acts 3.20.
6 Luke 15.20.
7 John Donne, 1572–1631, sermon, 'God's Mercies'.
8 Fred Benson describing his mother Mary Benson, in Rodney Bolt, *As Good as God, as Clever as the Devil*, London: Atlantic Books, 2011, p. 136.
9 'Praise, my soul, the king of heaven', by Henry Francis Lyte, 1793–1847.
10 Ps. 65.9.
11 Ps. 42.7.
12 Rom. 6.3.

3

CLOTHED

'Here we are clothed with Christ.'
Common Worship:
Christian Initiation: Holy Baptism, Introduction

'Quickly, bring out a robe – the best one – and put it on
him; put a ring on his finger and sandals on his feet.'
Luke 15.22

The second aspect of baptism that the president reminds us of at the outset is that of being clothed with Christ, 'dying to sin that we may live his risen life'. In this age of designer clothes, Jesus is our label.

A recurring nightmare for many people involves turning up at a special function in the wrong outfit, or even no outfit at all, being stared at by everyone present as the one person in the room incorrectly dressed or even stark naked. Jesus uses such an incident at a wedding reception in one of his stories about the kingdom.[1] We are required to be dressed for the occasion.

I once managed to live out the nightmare in spectacular fashion at a national conference, having failed to read the small print specifying for the men a dark suit and tie for the banquet. Alone among 300 diners there I sat in my sports jacket, squirming in my seat, trying to make myself even smaller than I already felt.

Clothing our nakedness was a theme that Paul took up when, writing to the church at Corinth, he speaks of 'longing to be clothed with our heavenly dwelling'.[2] No surprise then that the first Christians should adopt the custom of clothing the newly baptized with a white robe to signify their new life in Christ. Whiteness symbolized purity and emergence from the fire of persecution; the church at Laodicea was counselled in the book of Revelation to obtain 'white robes to clothe you and to keep the shame of your nakedness from being seen'.[3]

Today, the new and reinvigorated liturgies of the Church have restored to us this ancient and expressive custom of re-clothing, and when the candidates emerge from the water the president wraps them with a white robe, announcing:

You have been clothed with Christ.
As many as are baptised have put on Christ.[4]

Although we are loath to admit it, there is something in most of us that enjoys dressing up. We know the power of formal attire, of uniform, to help make us who we are. Once we are kitted out properly we pull ourselves up to full height, sneak a view in the mirror, and declare to ourselves (but certainly to no one else) that we don't look too bad. We enter the room with our confidence boosted, feeling good.

So it is that the newly baptized, clothed anew both physically and spiritually, are able to enter with confidence into the full life of the assembly, to take their rightful place at the table. But we first try on our new clothes alone, in the privacy of our own room, excitedly and a little nervously. We must make sure they fit before we sally forth.

Jesus emphasized that the life of prayer starts with us; like charity, it begins at home. 'Whenever you pray', he taught, 'go into your room and shut the door and pray to your father who is in secret.'[5] When we enter into the life of Christ we begin quietly and privately, testing how this new way feels, what difference it makes to how we see things, how we react and respond. Once we feel comfortable with the newness we can make our way eagerly and joyfully to join the others in the assembly of God's people. Here we shall no longer feel self-conscious or different, for we shall be one of a countless throng, journeying together, all of us re-clothed in Christ.

'Let all Christians regard their baptism as the daily garment that they are to wear all the time', urged Martin Luther,[6] and the baptismal life is one of daily remembering who we are. Paul affirmed that 'if anyone is in Christ, there is a new creation: everything old has passed away; see, everything has become new!'[7] Our call requires us to do what leopards cannot: change our spots. By the grace of God we become a new kind of person, refashioned in the pattern of Jesus, living to our full potential, discovering what it means to be completely and gloriously human.[8]

Our being clothed with Christ reminds us that it is the baptismal call that is paramount for every Christian. Compared with baptism, all other particular roles or tasks in the Church – whether ordained or not – are secondary. Differences of function only emerge when we gather to offer worship or deliberate as a body. Then our respective roles come into focus, but at all other times we are first and foremost the community of the baptized. Baptism is the great leveller; together we are all ministers of Christ,[9] from the bishop to the newly baptized just emerging from the water.

In a picture of life in the early, persecuted Church transposed to contemporary London, Gregory Dix[10] creates an imaginary setting of the Eucharist in which distinctions other than baptism are of little account. He describes how participants move quietly through the empty streets at first light to a prohibited meeting

at a secret location, the house of one of their wealth-
ier fellow members. Sunday is an ordinary working
day and they are all in their everyday clothes, and not
until they are all assembled around the table does it
emerge who's who. Only then is the man who 'looked
like a bank manager' revealed as the bishop, and the
liturgy can begin.

Spiritually speaking there is more than one layer
to our new suit of clothes, and our underwear – our
foundation garment – is humility. 'Clothe yourselves
with humility in your dealings with one another',
urged the author of 1 Peter.[11] Though today we would
frown at the notion of the hair shirt – worn next to
the skin to remind the wearer constantly of human
frailty – nevertheless a proper humility is appropriate
and obligatory dress.

We need to be reminded at every move of our fragil-
ity and of God's mercy to us, so that we may be slow
to pass judgement on others. Having a real grasp of
our indebtedness to God, remembering what we were,
and what we have become in Christ, keeps our pride
in check and our sense of the ridiculous in good trim.

A builder who once did some repairs to our vicar-
age recounted a visit to another parish where he had

enquired after 'Fr Smith', only to be corrected rather sharply that surely he meant 'Canon Smith'. Oops! Someone had forgotten to put on their baptismal robe that day, let alone their hair shirt.

Upon the foundation garment of humility, other layers can be wrapped around us to warm and protect us, and brighten the lives of others. The Focolare Movement is one of a number of institutes that have sprung up in the contemporary Church to help us rethink what it means to be consecrated to God in today's world. Its founder, Chiara Lubich, always said that the Movement's members should be distinguished not by the wearing of a religious habit but by putting on each day 'the habit of joy'.[12]

One member of our local church is a person recognized and known by her smile. She explains that her father, a worker in the Tyneside shipyards, taught her always to smile, saying that she would be repaid a hundredfold. She stands out in the crowd as a person of grace, ready to help, ready to instinctively say 'yes'. This is her habit of joy, her baptismal robe worn daily.

There are times also when specialist gear is required: an apron for cooking, gardening gloves for pulling nettles. The author of the letter to the church at Ephesus used the armour worn by soldiers as a metaphor of the spiritual protection needed by followers of Christ in difficult times. The times are critical and the appropriate clothing now is battle armour: 'Stand therefore, and fasten the belt of truth about your waist, and put on the breastplate of righteousness.'[13]

In our own generation in the West, Christians face problems, both in society and in the Church, as serious as those of the first centuries. The clothing of truth, and righteousness, and salvation, and the Spirit, enumerated in the letter to the Ephesians, will need to be strapped tightly around us, like bandages around the aching limb of an athlete, that we may stay ready and equipped.

It is, however, the white baptismal robe that distinguishes the faithful servants of Christ and clothes them in splendid apparel. The book of Revelation, whose vivid but violent imagery bears witness to the ordeal of the Church's birth pangs, has the last word when it comes to white robes.

In the midst of barbaric persecution, the Christian community that produced this apocalyptic work kept their hopes alive with a dazzling vision of heaven in which death and suffering is no more, all wrongs are righted, and every tear wiped from their eyes.[14] In this vision, the symbolic figures of 24 elders dressed in white robes and wearing golden crowns loom large.[15] On enquiring as to their identity, the narrator is told, 'These are they who have come out of the great ordeal; they have washed their robes and made them white in the blood of the Lamb.'[16]

This dramatic and highly coloured language may sound strange to our ears but contains a deep truth about the life of those called to be baptized into Christ's death. When James and John came to Jesus asking for special seats when it was all over, he questions whether they are willing to undergo what he is to undergo, drinking the same cup and being baptized with the same baptism.[17]

There is more than a ritual washing alluded to here; Jesus is asking James and John if they are able to enter into his own baptism of fire, into his ordeal. He asks this too of all those who seek baptism, and we must ponder our readiness.

James and John were quick to answer 'yes', but they had little idea of what they were saying, unaware that all but one of the Twelve were to die a violent death also. This was to be their own baptism of fire, through which they would be numbered among the 24 elders of the vision of Revelation, dressed in white robes, crowned and seated in the kingdom of heaven. White robes, then, are not just for babies, but for heroes.

Notes

1 Matt. 22.1–14.
2 2 Cor. 5.2: 'For in this tent we groan, longing to be clothed with our heavenly dwelling – if indeed, when we have taken it off we will not be found naked.'
3 Rev. 3.18.
4 *Common Worship: Christian Initiation*, p. 71.
5 Matt. 6.6.
6 Martin Luther, *The Large Catechism*, 1529.
7 2 Cor. 5.17.
8 'The glory of God is man fully alive.' Irenaeus, 130–200 CE, *Against Heresies*, Bk, 4, 20, 5–7.
9 One reason why we should avoid referring to the ordained clergy as 'ministers', for we all are.
10 Gregory Dix, *The Shape of the Liturgy*, London: Dacre Press, 1945.
11 1 Pet. 5.5.
12 Chiara Lubich, 1920–2008.
13 Eph. 6.14.
14 Rev. 21.4.
15 Rev. 4.4.
16 Rev. 7.14.
17 Mark 10.38.

4

GROWING TO FULL STATURE

'. . . and grow into the full stature of your Son, Jesus Christ.'
Common Worship:
Christian Initiation: Holy Baptism, The Collect

A mustard seed . . . is the smallest among all seeds,
but when it has grown it is the greatest of shrubs and
becomes a tree, so that the birds of the air come and
make nests in its branches.
Matthew 13.32

The collect at the beginning of a celebration of baptism and confirmation prays that all who are given new birth in Christian Initiation may 'grow into the full stature' of Jesus, God's anointed one. This puts growing up high on the agenda of those following the Way.

'Why be born again when you can just grow up?' was a question asked of Jack Reacher[1] by his father, who unwittingly put his finger on a tension within the Christian life between the moment and the process.

No matter how we come to faith – blinding flash or slow dawning – sooner or later we must knuckle down to some serious growing up. Like new arrivals from overseas, our baptism and confirmation get us through immigration and customs, but that's just the start. We have a new country to explore, a new language to learn, and a new culture to become part of. Growing up into Christ is a lifetime's work. We wear our L-plate to the grave.

Like children on the first morning of a seaside holiday, we can't wait to get going, and are out before breakfast finding the path down to the beach. The Christian Way is a rich mosaic of countless insights and traditions, of methods of prayer, patterns of worship and models of discipleship and communal living, and there is so much for us to explore, to discover, to read, to study, to dig for and open up like buried treasure. Gradually we discover more about the wonder of God, what works best for us, and how best we can help make a difference.

The scriptures will be our starting point: not diving in blind, which could be off-putting, but using the resources available to set them in context and interpret them for today. Reading plans with sets of daily notes are readily available, or we may prefer to use the passages of scripture selected by the Church for morning and evening prayer, which will lead us into a daily pattern for our spiritual life.

As we dig deeper, we will seek out further reading; perhaps books about how the scriptures were put together and who wrote them, or lives of the saints and influential Christians today, or authors who will help develop our spiritual understanding and prayer life. There is a mountain of available material but not all of it will be sound and sensible, for any road of faith can be subject to distortion and lack of balance. For this reason it is wise to seek advice on where to start and how to progress from those trained and authorized to lead in our own community of faith, whose approach we have come to trust.

A reliable and trustworthy guide is a godsend whenever we travel, no more so than on the journey of life. A spiritual director plays a vital role in the development of one's spiritual life, and tracking down a suitable person will be a priority. This role is best exercised by someone one step removed from our regular routine – neither friend nor parish clergy – who is experienced in the field of spiritual guidance and who can help us stand back and see the direction of our lives. Our spiritual director may also be our confessor – someone who guides us through the sacrament of reconciliation at regular intervals – but these roles are not necessarily combined. An annual time of retreat from the hurly-burly, enjoying the luxury of time alone before God, is another essential ingredient of a well-balanced spiritual regimen, and something we may do with our parish community or on our own.[2]

Because the Christian life is at base a communal rather than individual venture, much of our training is inevitably done together with others, as part of the community of faith which Paul, in a stroke of genius, named 'the body of Christ'.[3] The letter to the

Christian community at Ephesus is the workbook of growing up into Christ, full of those little gems of wisdom useful for sticking on the fridge door. When the author describes the gifts of God's Spirit that 'equip the saints for the work of ministry, for building up the body of Christ,'[4] he explains that this is an ongoing process through which we grow to our full height, 'until all of us come . . . to maturity, to the measure of the full stature of Christ'.[5]

These gifts of the Spirit are not given for our personal edification or spiritual aggrandizement but for the good of the whole community, so that we might 'grow up in every way . . . into Christ'.[6] Then, and only then, will we be able to play our proper part, knit together like ligaments of the body, promoting 'the body's growth in building itself up in love'.[7] The assembly of God's people *works* as a place of nurture because it is a place where love is found, a culture in which new life is rejoiced in and tenderly cared for and encouraged. I am hopeless at maths largely because I was made to feel a fool by a teacher who threw the blackboard rubber at pupils who got the answer wrong. Love, not fear, is the climate in which we relax enough to learn.

The author Maeve Binchy recalled how as a child she was 'fat and hopeless at games, but very happy because her parents thought all their geese were swans'.[8] This unwavering and unconditional love gave her total security and the confidence to feel that anything she wanted to achieve was possible. In the community of faith, too, all God's children are swans.

Since acquiring an allotment I have rediscovered the astonishing power of new growth in nature, but also the need for structure by which growth is sustained and directed. Like the wigwam of canes for the runner beans, which gives individual plants shape and direction, the assembly of God's people is the structure in which we can find space to grow and develop into the fullness of humanity embodied for us in Jesus, the Christ of God.

When we gather each week to build a community of faith, we are like young shoots, bursting with new life and energy but needing a framework in which to grow. Each of us will bring to the table our own enthusiasm, our own experience of the Way so far, our own tips for daily living in Christ. As we make Eucharist, pray together and study the scriptures, as we share meals in one another's homes, as we do jobs, have fun, deal with conflict, make peace, share loads, we are using to the full the framework that enables us to grow to our full height and potential.

Paul at times despaired of the infant church at Corinth for its continuing dependence on milk rather than solid food.[9] They were capable of so much more, but refused to grasp hold of the frame and pull themselves upwards, content to flounder. Their inability to be weaned off baby food was evidenced in their jealousies, quarrelling and party strife, behaviour which, then as now, disfigures the body of Christ and strips us of our credentials as people of good news.

Adolescence is not always an easy stage or a pretty sight, and immature churches will behave in much the same way as teenagers: demanding and dependent, unwilling to learn, and slow to consider the needs of others. Immature churches may seem fine at first sight, but on closer acquaintance are revealed as environments that keep us earthbound instead of giving us wings to fly. Their God remains small.[10]

Sometimes we may get discouraged on the way, but should never lose heart. In every congregation there will be men and women of faith, quietly plugging away, open to change, eager for new life. Like Simeon and

Anna waiting in the temple,[11] they are people on whom the Spirit rests and who long for the kingdom of God. These are our co-workers in creating mature communities of faith fit for the sons and daughters of God.

Paul encourages the community at Corinth to keep on growing by telling them that 'when I became an adult I put an end to childish ways'.[12] Maturity means that we are aware of our shortcomings and our need to grow, emboldened to experiment and explore, especially in the way we refashion and re-present the life of faith to a hungry world.

The tradition of referring to God as a male of the human species, for example, not only jars with contemporary culture but cramps our understanding of the One, beyond imagining, in whom the limitless creation as yet only glimpsed by humankind is held in being. Continually we need to grow and re-express and reconceptualize our vision of the unknowable source of life, even as we become more aware, not less, that every attempt to define or delineate will remain hopelessly inadequate.

Over the last 100 years there has been a massive turning away from religious observance in Western Europe in the face of unparalleled global conflict and catastrophe, and advances in scientific knowledge. In the face of the apparent randomness of evil, the notion of an all-powerful and merciful God appears more and more untenable,[13] and the Church marginalized and impotent.

The picture of God pieced together in Sunday school has been found wanting, but the Church has been slow to retool for its new task in a changed world. Are we honest or mature enough to offer a more robust picture of God, who participates in our brokenness? The language of worship all too often perpetuates the image of an all-mighty God who controls events, rather than of God-with-us, who suffers with us, and who enfolds us in love through the worst that evil can do, as in the story of Jesus himself.

We follow a Son of Man whose ministry of new life, healing and reconciliation ended in a brutal public execution. If there were no special deals for Jesus, even when he prayed in Gethsemane that his likely fate might be avoided,[14] then we cannot suppose it will be any different for us if we follow him in his radical and subversive programme to establish the kingdom of God.[15] As Thomas said, 'Let us also go, that we may die with him.'[16]

And yet, as soon as we think we might have to let go of the traditional picture of the interventionist God, the amazing coincidence (or God-incidence) of paths converging, or of beautiful things happening against odds of millions to one, stops us in our tracks. It would take 100,000 years, travelling at the speed of light, to cross our universe, yet at times the life force that holds together this immense, unimaginable creation appears to exercise a tender care for each one of us, personal and precise. We see that the 'universe is sustained by a continual and infinitely patient act of love'.[17]

Growing into the full stature of Christ requires us to live with the unknowing. No longer demanding answers, or neat solutions, we become mature enough to live with provisionality and uncertainty. In his final days Jesus 'set his face to go to Jerusalem',[18] not knowing what would befall him there. It is there that we seek him out and walk with him.

Notes

1 The creation of Lee Child, master of suspense thrillers, Jack Reacher is a hero for our times, a latter-day Robin Hood, confronting wrong wherever he finds it. A man of few words but the occasional pithy saying.

2 The Association for Promoting Retreats publishes a useful guide to the many centres available across the UK <www.promotingretreats.org>.

3 1 Cor. 12.27.

4 Eph. 4.12.

5 Eph. 4.13.

6 Eph. 4.15.

7 Eph. 4.16.

8 Maeve Binchy, 1940–2012, Obituary, *Guardian*, 2 August 2012.

9 1 Cor. 3.1–3.

10 But we make his love too narrow
By false limits of our own;
And we magnify his strictness
With a zeal he will not own.
From 'There's a wideness in God's mercy' by Frederick William Faber, 1814–63.

11 Luke 2.25–38.

12 1 Cor. 13.11.

13 Rabbi Harold Kushner's book *When Bad Things Happen to Good People* was the first of several on this theme, and proved a best-seller because it addressed the question that everyone asks.

14 So hard that 'his sweat became like great drops of blood falling onto the ground' (Luke 22.44).

15 Chad Myers, *Binding the Strong Man*, Maryknoll, NY: Orbis, 1991, p. 186.
16 John 11.16.
17 Francis Spufford, *Guardian*, 2 September 2012.
18 Luke 9.51.

5

DRAWING BY EXAMPLE

'Draw them by your example into the community of faith.'
Common Worship: Christian Initiation:
Holy Baptism, Presentation of the Candidates

So if I, your Lord and Teacher, have washed your feet,
you also ought to wash one another's feet.
For I have set you an example, that you also should do
what I have done to you.
John 13.14–15

In the baptismal liturgy the president asks those who bring candidates to baptism whether they will be faithful in praying for them and will draw them into a full life in the Christian community by their own example. One good and inspiring example speaks louder than a thousand words of advice.

When we think back to our schooldays, the people we remember with affection and lasting gratitude are those who opened windows onto the world for us, who didn't just teach us, but changed our lives. They were memorable not just for their imparting of knowledge, but for the way they lived life. Their personalities and manner were so attractive that we wanted to learn from them, wanted to be with them. They drew us by their example.

My love of mountains was fostered by Messrs Barnes and Edwards, two dedicated teachers at my Small Heath school. They took a group of us sixth-formers for a week's fell-walking, staying in converted miners' cottages in the shadow of the Lakeland peak known as Coniston Old Man. New kingdoms were discovered and conquered, and I can taste the summit prize of tinned grapefruit to this day.

Through their own commitment and dedication, our teachers made of our disregarded school (we were, after all, co-ed and played only soccer), 'a brash and noble container of dreams . . . a beacon of optimism, a dynamo of energy'.[1] We wanted to grow up to be like them, and to change lives, as they had done.

In his memoirs Ferdinand Mount describes the greatest teacher he ever knew, the philosopher J. L. Austin, who was listened to with an intentness never known before or since. When he strode from the room at the end of the lecture, 'the hush remained unbroken for a minute or two, as though we had been holding our breath for the whole hour, and had forgotten how to breathe out'.[2]

Jesus was a teacher of unparalleled authority and mesmeric power. The people crowded round, pushing and shoving. They climbed trees, sat on roofs, removed tiles, just to get a glimpse, just to hear a word. Here is a person who never compelled or persuaded others. He simply arrived, stood to speak, said what he had to say, and allowed everyone to come to their own conclusion. 'Let anyone with ears listen!'[3] was a favourite saying. He drew others to him, never dragged or drove them.

This is why what we do when we meet together to be made Church is of immense significance. Our worship is more important than anything else we do. It is the shop window of our life together, at which the passer-by will pause for a moment before either walking on by or coming in to take a closer look.

One of the special joys of the Christian life is helping to create worship that will not only give glory to God but cause the casual visitor to stop, look and listen. Such worship will be a work of art, a sculpture in words, music and movement, faithfully representing to the best of our ability the wondrous mystery of God among us. It has to blow us away. In this process of worship we are moulded and knocked into shape, to become salt, and leaven, and light for the world.

A mark of good worship will be theological integrity; what it says on the label is what you get. If we say we are a pilgrim community, do we *look* like pilgrims on a journey or a bunch of people stuck to our seats? If we say we are participants rather than observers, do we gather *around* what is happening, or line up in front of it like an audience waiting for the show to begin? If we speak of being a community, do we sit close together, in relationship with each other, or scatter ourselves across acres of empty pews? If we say we are a single, united body, are we willing to gather 'all together in one place' like the crowd at the first Pentecost,[4] happy to muck in together, rubbing shoulders with all sorts and all styles, that the common good might prevail over personal preference?

In tussling with these issues, the body of Christ is built up and grows into maturity, and in so doing we practise and hone our 'drawing skills', our 'practice of the presence of God',[5] enabling us to draw others irresistibly into the company of those who walk the way of Jesus.

When Andrew and his companion first encountered Jesus, they asked him where he was staying. His response was, 'Come and see.'[6] Dare we say those words? Our worship has to be wondrous enough for us to be able to speak those words with utter confidence that those who respond will not be disappointed.

What will draw others more than anything is love. Not the soft and sentimental kind, but the kind that Jesus embodied in his living and dying: total, unconditional, costly. Paul reminds us that when it comes to living a godly life as followers of Jesus, love is the supreme virtue that puts all others in the shade. The gifts we imagine to be so important, from faith itself to good works and all kinds of spiritual accomplishments, are not just secondary to love; without love they are invalidated.[7]

When we gather to worship as the people of God, order and beauty and excellence will not be enough if we wish to be a community of transformation drawing others into belonging and faith. What we must become is a community of God's love, so wonderful and captivating and true that we find ourselves willing to let go of everything else just to be part of it. The impact of Jesus' presence was such that his first followers 'immediately left their nets and followed him'.[8] We need to work at creating worship with a similar drawing power. Philip Larkin, in his poem 'An Arundel Tomb', gazes at a medieval tomb of a nobleman and his lady, two figures lying with hands clasped, their dogs at their feet, and ponders their life together. After all this time, what do they say to us? He concludes with the line, 'What will survive of us is love.'[9] So too for us; no matter what worship is offered, or growth occurs, or projects or programmes are developed, what will survive of our faith community, in the final analysis, is love.

On the north-west side of Wasdale in the Western Lakes there is a beautiful mountain shaped like an upturned boat, called Yewbarrow. It's not the highest in the vicinity, but the most alluring. It draws you, nay compels you, to climb it. So one day I did. When afterwards I read Wainwright's definitive guide, I found that I had in blissful ignorance scaled a summit he classifies as 'difficult of attainment' and therefore 'not often climbed'. Although he rates Stirrup Crag, at the summit, 'as nothing more than a strenuous exercise in elementary gymnastics and unusual postures', he says that those who come after might be able to follow his trail of blood.[10] No wonder the two experienced fell-walkers I met in the car park afterwards called it 'a toughie'. I felt a glow of achievement, but realized that had I known all this beforehand, I would never have dared attempt it.

Worship, like fell-walking, should at times take us beyond our comfort zone. Always to play it safe will leave us feeling dissatisfied and unfulfilled, cocooned in our comfort blanket. At least sometimes, we need something a bit beyond us, something that pushes us to the limit, that includes just a hint of danger. Worship should be at the same time familiar and enjoyable, but breathtaking and a little scary; just now and then

'a toughie'. Worship that engages, inspires and trans-
forms will contain an element of that which is always
just beyond our reach, propelling us further than we
are normally willing to go. It should leave us breath-
less at our own audacity in venturing into unexplored
territory, reaching for the very gate of heaven. It is
this sense of excitement that will make others want
to join us, to come with us to the top.

The Philadelphia-based musician and composer
Bobby McFerrin says that making music is not merely
a question of hitting the right notes in the correct
sequence. 'I suddenly realized', he says, 'that to really
make music you had to bare your heart and soul. You
had to take a trip into the unknown.'[11]

Worship, if it is to draw and beguile and enchant,
should have about it a mysterious and challenging
quality which at the same time fills us with fear and
trembling yet beckons us irresistibly onward into
areas yet to be discovered and relished.

While the pattern of regular worship, the shape of
the liturgy, the framework of the Mass, will remain
familiar and reassuring, there should always be room
for God's spirit to leap out at us to take us by surprise. In worship, at least sometimes, we should be

amazed at what we find ourselves doing – things that, if known beforehand, might have caused us to turn back. Whenever we consider ourselves to be completely in charge of worship, when we have it screwed down, we shall run the risk of reducing an encounter with the living God to the mere recitation of words on a page. Total predictability and security make for inadequate worship, leaving us feeling a little empty, or plain bored. Good worship lifts us to places we haven't been to before, astonishing us by the spectacle of the extraordinary pouring forth from the ordinary and mundane.

When we get ready for church on Sunday, do we see it as a stroll through familiar territory, a venture into the unknown, or a bit of both? Unless *we* think the journey worthwhile and the goal indescribably wonderful, it is unlikely that others will follow.

A Tyneside parishioner who helped me by her example was a lady in her nineties who never lost her sense of excitement at the possibilities of worship. 'I wonder what will be different at church this Sunday?' she used to ask her daughter as they walked down the street. 'Whatever it is, I know it will be good.' She had it about right.

Notes

1 Peter Jennings, 1938–2005, Canadian-born television journalist and anchor man, describing in a newspaper interview what his adopted home, the USA, meant to him.

2 Ferdinand Mount, *Cold Cream*, London: Bloomsbury, 2009, p. 179.

3 Matt. 11.15; 13.9; Mark 4.9, 23.

4 Acts 2.1.

5 The title of a Christian spiritual classic by Brother Laurence (Nicholas Herman), 1605–91.

6 John 1.39.

7 1 Cor. 13.1–3.

8 Mark 1.18.

9 Philip Larkin, 'An Arundel Tomb', *The Whitsun Weddings*, London, Faber and Faber, 1964.

10 Alfred Wainwright, *The Western Fells*, London: Frances Lincoln, 2003.

11 Bobby McFerrin, *Guardian*, 7 May 2010.

6

TAKING OUR PLACE

'. . . and help them to take their place within the life and
worship of Christ's Church.'
*Common Worship: Christian Initiation:
Holy Baptism, Presentation of the Candidates*

But when you are invited, go and sit down at the lowest
place, so that when your host comes, he may say to you,
'Friend, move up higher'; then you will be honoured
in the presence of all who sit at table with you.
Luke 14.10

Those bringing candidates for baptism, having promised to lead by example, are also asked by the president whether they will care for those they sponsor and help them to take the place that awaits them at the table of God.

When you find an empty chair in a room full of people and ask, 'Anyone sitting here?', the very best reply of all is 'Yes: you are!' Here is no grudging response but the warmest of welcomes. They may never have seen you before in their lives, but they speak as if you were expected, and needed, already part of the seating plan.

When we gather as the holy assembly of God's people, we welcome each other in the same way. There is no such thing as a reserved seat, a seat saved for someone else. Any spare seat is *your* seat, where your presence is expected and looked forward to, and delighted in. The holy assembly models for us the kingdom of God, where each person is valued, held in honour. A place is ready for us at the table, with our own place card beautifully inscribed. We are those honoured guests to whom God says, 'everything is ready; come'.[1] This invitation is echoed intentionaly and powerfully in the liturgy when, after the gifts of bread and wine have been placed on the altar table, the president reminds the assembly that we are here at Jesus' invitation, as honoured guests: 'The people will come from east and west, from north and south, and will eat in the kingdom of God. Come, you that are blessed by my Father, inherit the kingdom prepared for you from the foundation of the world. Come for everything is ready.'[2]

We glimpse in that moment exactly who we are: God's children and co-workers with Christ. We participate at this feast not as deprived recipients of a welfare programme but as the beloved sons and daughters of the king, taking our rightful place beside him. We have come home.

Sometimes we also come down with a bump at this point, if the gap between our expectation and the reality of Sunday morning is too great. Eagerly looking forward to taking our place in a liturgy in which all will participate, we find ourselves instead ushered into a pew a long way from the action and a safe distance from any other worshipper. Surely there is more to it than this?

But go to the little medieval church of St John the Baptist, Winchester – just one example of countless reordered churches up and down the country – and you will be welcomed immediately into a company of pilgrims who gather in order to make worship happen. The nave floor has been cleared of pews, and chairs are set in two elliptical curves, either side of the ambo (lectern) and altar table. The foci of worship are immediate, not up steps or behind screens, and everyone is part of the action.

Difficulties arise because the rooms in which we worship will more often than not be hand-me-downs from a previous era. Glorious and inspirational though they may be, they will nevertheless impact on our ability to offer worship that is appropriate for our own generation. They were designed for people who lived in a very different world, and tend to give us separation when we want oneness, steps where we need a level space, and barriers when we need to see and participate fully. Often we are prevented by the sheer volume of furniture crammed into the space from getting near to the altar table and must instead gaze at it from afar.

For the newly baptized, the details of church history may seem daunting and perhaps irrelevant, but they are nevertheless helpful in understanding what we do today and why.[3] No worship space is neutral, but bears witness to how we approached things in previous generations. The parish church where I grew up bore the scars, in the form of smashed monuments and sword-marks scouring the walls, of religious extremism of former centuries, and taught me much about who we were and where we had come from. As we become more familiar with the scriptures and with the story of the Church's development, we gradually acquire the 'theological spectacles' through which to observe and ponder not just the past, but what is going on around us today.

As our experience of the Christian Way deepens, we may begin to look beyond the external details of the building and the order of service to ask, 'What is happening here?' We might become adept at spotting intrusive barriers from a bygone age and habits of worship that no longer have meaning, and perhaps motivated to play our part in making things better, renewing our shared liturgical life in the process. As churches grow in maturity of faith we hunger for a more complete expression of our equality and interdependence in Christ, determined to let nothing detract from the glorious unity of the holy assembly of God's people.

We may be only a single voice, but should never underestimate the contribution of the new member to recall, by the freshness of their faith, the whole community to its first love. Into the newcomer's hands can be given the ministry of asking questions – sometimes the apparently 'stupid' question – which bring the rest of us up with a jolt, requiring the whole body to re-examine what it does and to do it even better.

Sometimes our questions may prompt the faith community to work more imaginatively with the spaces we have, or experiment with other spaces at our disposal, whether church hall, or local school, or coffee shop. At other times we may find ourselves part of an exciting project to completely rethink and reorder our worship space, to provide a spiritual home worthy of our aspirations and revitalize our community.

The details matter less than the process by which we are caught up in the rediscovery of our true identity as God's people and the work of worship entrusted to us, proclaiming that holy things and holy places belong to holy people, which means every single one of us. Here we may experience with renewed excitement the Church's primitive nature and essential unity as a community of the baptized, exercising the priestly call of God's people.[4]

In line with this rediscovery, our habits of worship will begin to emphasize the communal rather than the personal, our unity rather than the privileges of office. The Sunday liturgy at Philadelphia Cathedral gives one of many examples of putting theory into practice. Here the whole assembly is seated at one level, and in the midst of the space stands the altar table – not on steps or behind a rail, but immediately accessible to God's people.

Following the Liturgy of the Word, the whole assembly makes its way to encircle the altar table, for the people offer their gifts and themselves to God, and to make the great prayer of thanksgiving over bread and wine known as the Eucharistic Prayer. Although the words of the prayer are spoken by the president, the whole assembly claims it for its own, to make it the prayer of all the ministers of the Eucharist – that is, every man, woman and child present. With heads erect and hands raised, we stand as a community who belong in the holy place, embodying the words of the prayer we proclaim: 'we thank you for counting us worthy to stand in your presence and serve you'.[5]

At communion, after the holy bread is administered to the assembly standing around the altar, each member is invited to approach the altar table to take into their own hands the cup of wine, for as the holy people of God we have no need of an intermediary. The president receives last, not first, of all, as befits a servant of the servants of God. These small gestures are telling signs of the kingdom.

In these ways the full significance of our baptismal life is revealed, and we are enabled to take our place at the table with confidence and joy. Our eyes are opened to what we truly are as members of the community of the baptized: 'we, who are many, are one body in Christ, and individually we are members one of another.'[6] Here we discover that we are no longer 'churchgoers' attending a service at which we may be inspired or edified or entertained by professionals up front, but a community of ministries gathering to *become* Church, to create and offer the liturgy, to be fully who we are in Christ.[7]

When boy meets girl, an important step in the relationship is the first proper meal together. This may involve a corner table for two at a special restaurant, or a meal at the family home where, armed with a bunch of flowers, the boy steels himself to undergo her mother's cooking and her father's questions.[8] The meal is the thing; it cements the relationship, it embodies acceptance.

No wonder, then, that the meal is central to the teaching of Jesus. More than just talk about it, Jesus used eating and drinking to symbolize his whole ministry, and to proclaim the kingdom of God. Because he chose to eat with 'the wrong people',[9] he reversed the priorities and pecking order of the world and embodied God's reckless unconditional hospitality. This is the radical programme we become part of when we take our place at the table of Jesus, in the tradition of the Apostles who were recognized as those 'who have been turning the world upside down'.[10]

In the Eucharist we are present not only in the room we occupy in the here and now, but also in the upper room with Jesus on his last night with his friends, on the shore of the lake, and on the road to Emmaus. And we not only look backward, but forward too, to the heavenly banquet that takes centre stage in the final book of the Christian scriptures.[11] So we come to understand that our making Eucharist in this world is merely a dry run for the real thing.

When we gather as the holy assembly round the altar table, we are just limbering up, getting our bodies and hearts and minds in shape so that we shall be fit to take part in the eternal feast in the new heavenly Jerusalem, where we shall take our place alongside all God's beloved. 'There, creation will be healed into paradise, and each and all of earth's children will be welcomed at the gate, embraced and kissed and ushered to a place at the table in that city of peace.'[12]

Notes

1 Matt. 22.4.
2 A conflation of Luke13.29, Matt. 25.34 and Matt. 22.4. This custom originated at St Gregory's San Francisco, as part of the inspirational programme of liturgical renewal led by Rick Fabian and Donald Schell. It was adopted by Philadelphia Cathedral and many other places.
3 The buildings in which we worship have been shaped by a 2,000-year-long process of liturgical development that has, for various reasons, tended to clutter the space and obscure the meaning of its chief components. Both Jewish temple and Roman basilica were influences that helped shape early Christian buildings, and combined to emphasize concepts of holiness and separation and

authority, which in turn were reinforced by the growing importance of the professional clergy as an elite who took care of worship for the rest of us. These questions are addressed more fully in *Re-pitching the Tent* (London: Canterbury Press, 2004).

4 The priesthood of the whole community (see 1 Pet. 2.4 and 9) is a very different concept from that of the 'priesthood of all believers' popular with the Reformers, which sought to bestow a priestly role on the individual.

5 'Eucharistic Prayer B', *Common Worship*, London: Church House Publishing, 2000.

6 Rom. 12.5.

7 One of the variants used at Philadelphia Cathedral for the giving of communion was a quotation from Augustine of Hippo: 'Receive what you are, the body of Christ.'

8 The 2011 film *Blue Valentine* includes a beautifully crafted and funny account of 'the first meal with the parents'.

9 He accepted invitations from Pharisees (Luke 14.1), lepers (Matt. 26.6), and those considered outcasts of society (Matt. 9.10). He set no boundaries to the hospitality of his table; even the prostitute who gatecrashed the meal with her jar of ointment must not be excluded (Luke 7.44–47).

10 Acts 17.6.

11 Rev. 19.9.

12 David Philippart, *Saving Signs, Wondrous Words*, Chicago: Liturgy Training Publications, 1996, p. 50.

7

SURRENDERING

'I turn to Christ . . . I submit to Christ . . . I come to Christ.'
Common Worship: Christian Initiation:
Holy Baptism, The Decision

But the tax collector, standing far off, would not even
look up to heaven, but was beating his breast and saying,
'God, be merciful to me, a sinner!'
Luke 18.13

In the Liturgy of Baptism, at the moment of Decision, the candidate promises to turn, to submit and to come to Christ. This is unqualified, stark language, redolent not of considering an idea, but of surrendering unconditionally. God asks us to hand over our lives, and we do.

I turn to Christ. Turning involves a change, of course, a turning off our previous path to strike out in a new direction, aiming for the goal clearly visible ahead. Often the well-trodden path is not the one we take; 'leave the main track at this point and strike off in a north-easterly direction', says the guide book, and although the main track looks reassuring, we trust our instincts and the experience of our guide, and go for it.

In baptism we leave the main track and follow the path of Christ. Jesus tells us beforehand that it is not the obvious route, wide and clearly marked, for 'the gate is narrow and the way is hard that leads to life, and there are few who find it'.[1]

In turning we are making a choice of direction that may cause us to relinquish much that we previously held dear, changing our mind on many issues. Although 'doing a U-turn' is much derided in political

life, changing one's mind can in fact require considerable courage. It can be the mark not of a weak, but
a great leader, someone who listens and learns and is
not afraid to accept that they may have been wrong.

In education or business, someone who turns things
around is someone who gives a school or a company
a completely new direction and image, transforming
a failing school or a loss-making concern into a highly
successful one, reinventing it in the process.

In baptism we turn around our lives, re-evaluating
the issues before us and reinventing ourselves in the
process. This involves not so much a repudiation of all
that has gone before, but a re-examination of our lives,
holding onto all that is good and true, and letting go
of those things that are now recognized as holding us
back or restricting our freedom to grow into the new
person we long to be in Christ.

And who do we turn *to*? We turn to Jesus, the Son
of Man, God's Anointed. Some Christian traditions we
encounter seem to teach propositions *about* Jesus –
who he is and what he does for us – rather than show
us Jesus himself. We are led to believe that if we say
certain things and go through certain motions we are
made all right with God, almost mechanically.

But Jesus is not a mantra to be repeated again and again, like some lucky charm to ward off evil. Jesus is a person we fall in love with and whose love is 'so amazing, so divine',[2] that we can do no other than follow him to the ends of the earth, without reservation or condition. 'Even though you do not see him now, you believe in him and rejoice with an indescribable and glorious joy.'[3]

If we genuinely attempt to follow in his footsteps, going where he went and on his terms, we shall discover that an early casualty is the 'absolute certainty' promised by fundamentalists at either end of the spectrum – those who insist on either sovereign scripture or sovereign church. In between these extremes lies the path of ceaseless exploration, valuing everything, in thrall to nothing. Jesus was absolutely certain of the love of God, and that alone. He gave no credence to the idea that we are 'safe' once we believe this or do that, and constantly warned his hearers – especially the religious ones – against presuming they had 'arrived'.[4]

With Jesus we live with uncertainty and without presumption. In his story of the Pharisee and tax collector praying at the temple, Jesus commends the heartfelt prayer of the tax collector, crying out in his wretchedness, not that of the self-righteous and con-fident Pharisee.[5] On the rough and rocky road trod-den by the companions of Jesus, staying upright and keeping on moving is work enough. This is no time for counting chickens.

We follow one whom Richard Holloway[6] calls 'the great outsider', the Son of Man who 'had nowhere to lay his head',[7] he who was 'counted among the lawless'.[8] When we as followers of this unpredict-able, unclassifiable, subversive teacher gather round the font at the beginning of our Sunday assembly, we plunge ourselves once again into the great adventure of tagging along after him.

I submit to Christ. When we talk of our submission to God, the example of our Muslim brothers and sisters immediately springs to mind. For them, surrendering to God is not a theory, but the essence of their faith. The very name 'Islam' translated into English means 'submission', and the Muslims' sense of surrender to God is their great gift to all their fellow pilgrims on the road to God.

It's probably fair to say that we in the West are not good at submission, and perhaps those of us mindful of belonging to a 'proud island race' find it more difficult than most. Submission is historically not our style, even when it comes to God. God is, after all, an English-man whom we feel free to address 'man to man', even delivering a good dressing-down on occasions – but that caricature of muscular Christianity is not what's written on the packet of the Way of Jesus.

Submission is often linked to the language of human conflict and warfare. One force conquers another and the vanquished foe submits to the superior power of his adversary. Submission of this kind is resented, and leaves a bitter taste. But if we look to the language of love, not war, all becomes clear. For when we fall in love we *long* to surrender; our only anxiety is lest the one we love won't *allow* us to, will show little or no interest in our white flag. In love, surrender comes easy. Submission is no hardship but our heart's desire.

Before we get to the point of submission, however, we may spend quite a while in futile evasion, fleeing the one who longs to embrace us. 'I fled him down the nights and down the days' is the opening line of Francis Thompson's famous poem 'The Hound of Heaven'.[9] We may start by running away from God, but there is no escape from God's love, and no peace until we have surrendered. 'Ah, fondest, blindest, weakest,' says the voice of God at the end of the poem, 'I am he whom thou seekest.' Only when we surrender shall we know peace of mind, for 'our hearts are restless' 'til they find their rest in You'.[10]

I come to Christ. 'Just coming!' is a child's cry familiar to every parent, a delaying tactic as old as the hills. We talk a lot about coming to God, but it's usually on our own terms, when it suits us, when we're ready. 'Give me chastity and continence, but not yet', was Augustine's famous prayer of delay,[11] but when we really long for something, or someone, it's an entirely different story.

On Sunday afternoons as a child I would keep watch at the front window of my grandparents' house (where I spent many weekends) so that I wouldn't miss sight of Dad at the wheel of the family car coming to pick us up. When the weather was good and my mother well enough, off we would go into the countryside, past Meriden down to Berkswell or Kenilworth, or even Henley-in-Arden for an ice cream.

When we come to living out our baptismal promises we learn again the joy of responding to God on

God's terms, not ours. When the one we long for is spotted through the window, we drop everything and run. We don't mess about making excuses. We don't need persuading or cajoling, for nothing will stop us. For this we have longed.

The most beautiful picture that the Gospels give us of God is found in Jesus' story of the two brothers.[12] The prodigal, wastrel brother who had blown his inheritance and was now destitute agonizes for months on whether he dare go back home to face his father. What could he possibly say, or do, to put things right? He practises his speech, going over and over what he will say. There is no other way, but he approaches with knocking knees, his rumbling stomach audible a mile off.

In Jesus' story, the father does not subject his wayward son to a cross-examination, or to a long wait on a seat in a corridor while a meeting with advisors decides his fate. No, as soon as he sees him approaching in the distance, the father rushes out across the fields to meet him: 'while he was still far off, his father saw him and was filled with compassion; he ran and put his arms around him and kissed him'. There is no standing on ceremony, no weighing of right or wrong, no recitation of faults, no recrimination. There is only rejoicing that this beloved though hapless child 'was dead and has come to life . . . was lost and has been found'.

Here is a God to whom we can surrender without hesitation, to whom we can submit without fear, to whom we can come without delay. This very week there may be ways in which we can test out our willingness to place ourselves in God's hands, and we should seek them out.

We need have no fear, for from the moment we make our first tiny step towards God, everything else is taken out of our hands; God beats us to it. As soon as we are caught sight of, dragging ourselves home, wounded and battered, broken and lost, and before we can utter a word, here is our loving, merciful, recklessly generous God, crying out, 'I come!'

Notes

1. Matt. 7.14.
2. Isaac Watts 1674–1748.
3. 1 Pet. 1.8.
4. Matt. 7.21–23; 21.31.
5. Luke 18.9–14.
6. Richard Holloway, Bishop of Edinburgh, 1986–2000.
7. Matt 8.20.
8. Luke 22.37.
9. Francis Joseph Thompson, 1859–1907.
10. Augustine of Hippo, *Confessions* I.1.
11. *Confessions* VIII.7.
12. Luke 15.11–32.

8

BEING EQUIPPED

'. . . the Spirit of wisdom and understanding . . . of counsel
and inward strength . . . of knowledge and true godliness.'
Common Worship: Christian Initiation: Confirmation

The gifts he gave were . . . to equip the saints for the work
of ministry, for building up the body of Christ.
Ephesians 4.11–12

Immediately before the act of confirmation, the bishop stretches his hands over the candidates and prays that God will touch and empower them with the characteristics named in both Hebrew and Christian scriptures as gifts of the Spirit of God.[1]

The gifts of the Spirit together form a package of qualities and attributes enabling the baptized to live a new kind of life. Because these gifts are so interrelated – one leading to, and proceeding from, another – there is much of the chicken-and-egg about them. It is hard to say which comes first. True godliness can be seen as both the fruit of these gifts and their starting point.

Experience of life tells us that our own version of these qualities tends to be second rate. Our limited wisdom is second hand, and never there when we want it, causing us to be wise well after the event. Our understanding is partial and bent out of shape by the accidents of upbringing and formation. Our counsel is often nothing more than soothing platitudes. As for knowledge, we recall William Blake's humbling stricture that 'all knowledge turns to lumber after two weeks'. In short we are in a sorry state, left to our own devices. We must start all over again with God.

Wisdom and understanding. 'Consider your own call', Paul says to the church at Corinth; 'not many of you were wise by human standards'.[2] We begin with an awareness of our own limitations in order to be re-equipped by the Spirit of God with a wisdom and understanding and knowledge not of our own making.

Indeed, wisdom as the world knows it gets a hammering in Paul's first letter to Corinth, as he derides the wisdom of the age for not having the sense to see what is under its nose. He sets the wisdom of the world over against the apparent 'foolishness' of the cross, and declares that 'God's foolishness is wiser than human wisdom.'[3]

So in placing ourselves under God in our baptismal life, we open up ourselves to receive wisdom and understanding of a different order. This is not the kind attained by the frantic cramming of information into our grey matter, but the kind that flows from our life with God in the company of those who walk with us on the journey of faith.

Neither is the wisdom and understanding spoken of here a one-off delivery of goodies at the bishop's hands, after which we can sit back and take it easy. Godly wisdom is acquired only through a lifetime of godliness, of waiting upon God. We learn awareness and watchfulness, knowing that the spiritual life can be easily skewed by the company we keep, the literature we read, the movements or pressure groups that impinge on our lives. The laying on of hands marks but the launch of a lifelong apprenticeship, a process in which we gradually assimilate ways of seeing and understanding things with the mind of Christ, for that is the incredible measure of the promise.[4]

'On God alone my soul in stillness waits', we read in the Psalms,[5] and our cultivation of a profound awareness of God's presence must begin deep within us. Unless we have peace within, no amount of external influence will be able to insert it for us. The baptismal life calls us to a continual opening of ourselves to God in the stillness of our own hearts, and in the stillness that falls upon the assembly gathered together before the holy mysteries.

Jesus invited his followers to 'Come away to a deserted place all by yourselves and rest awhile',[6] and regular times apart – moments in our regular routine and longer periods on retreat – will soon become a joy rather than a duty, inviolate in the diary, fiercely guarded.

The pursuit of wisdom and understanding begins with us, but doesn't end there, for this journey is no solo venture. Our own 'inner voice' must be checked out with the others in the community of faith; cross-referenced with what the community is saying now and what it has said in previous generations. The insights of other faith traditions are a further resource by which we can discern paths of wisdom and understanding all the stronger for being shared experience.

Unhurriedness is a consistent ally in acquiring wisdom. The tight deadline, the demands of others, the expectations of those above us or those for whom we are responsible, often conspire to pressure us into over-hasty decision-making. We are too quick in our judgements, jumping on bandwagons before checking which way they are heading.

Sometimes those bent on a course of wrongdoing or harm to others will look to the Christian for a seal of approval before going ahead, or dare us to defy them. It will take all our courage to stand alone, whether a conscientious objector at a time of war, or a lone voice in a group of friends making cruel fun of another.

True wisdom is a storehouse of experience applied to everyday living. Its discernment requires us to take one step back, withdrawing from the fray and quietening the hasty instinctive response, in order to draw conclusions that are calm and measured.

Counsel and inward strength. These gifts of the Spirit are evidenced whenever we embrace the cause of goodness and truth, particularly when we stand alone. All our inward strength will be required on those occasions when we find ourselves in a minority of one, raising our voice against a popular but wrong-headed course of action. The crowd swept by emotion can be a dangerous force, and the mob in hot pursuit a frightening sight. Søren Kierkegaard[7] was right in discerning that 'wherever the crowd is, there is untruth'.[8]

Joseph of Arimathea modelled inward strength when he summoned the courage to go and ask Pontius Pilate for the body of Jesus after his crucifixion. Worse even than the risk of approaching an all-powerful and capricious commander of an army of occupation was the irrevocable step he took in defying every other member of his respected peer group, the Jewish council. 'Though a member of the council', Joseph 'had not agreed to their plan and action.'[9] He was willing to go it alone because, we are told, 'he was waiting expectantly for the kingdom of God'. He kept his own counsel, and did the good and courageous thing.

Knowledge and true godliness. The artist Samuel Palmer[10] described how he once accompanied the visionary William Blake to an exhibition at the Royal Academy: 'there was Blake, he recalled, in his plain black suit . . . standing so quietly among all the dressed-up, rustling, swelling people, and myself thinking "How little you know *who* is among you!"'[11]

How little they knew who was among them in first-century Galilee. When Jesus was teaching, especially when his message was hard to take, he would often issue his 'take it or leave it' challenge.[12] He wept over the holy city of Jerusalem for its failure to have 'recognized on this day the things that make for peace'.[13] Everyone has ears, and eyes, but not many actually hear and see. This is the secret of the gift of knowledge and true godliness.

Arriving at Manchester airport late one night, after a five-hour flight delay, my wife and I were disconsolate at having watched the last train to Newcastle disappear into the distance. Our hearts sank further when we were joined by a youth with numerous body piercings, wearing studded leather and heavy boots, who looked as if he were on his way to mug a granny.

Great was our surprise when he gave us a broad smile, cheerfully enquiring, 'Have you been on holiday? Somewhere nice?' He proceeded to minister to us in our woe, assuring us that we won't have been the first people to have missed a train, and even offered to come with us if we needed to find a Metro tram. When our paths diverged we thanked this angel of God warmly for his care. Shame on us for our judging by appearances! Jesus is always there if we look long and hard enough.

Paul called such insight 'the discernment of spirits',[14] and here it is that the wisdom of true godliness really counts. By the Spirit of God we are enabled to glimpse, at least momentarily, the things around us through his eyes. We stand back from the crowd, recognizing the true meaning and import of what's going on, poking beneath the surface of things to get their true measure and meaning. We are led to see who it is who stands before us, and the potential for good in every situation. In so doing we are equipped to build communities of integrity, honesty and love.

The spiritual gifts bestowed in Christian Initiation don't come with a set of printed instructions. We shall need to try them out, gingerly at first but with growing confidence, exploring our capabilities and the nature of the ministries entrusted to us. We shall need to compare notes with others as to how best to use these gifts for the good of the whole body of Christ. Overenthusiasm may on occasions lead to our getting things wrong, but God loves a cheerful trier, and the worse sin is to let gifts lie dormant and unused.[15]

At confirmation the bishop prays on behalf of the candidates that 'their delight shall be in the fear of the Lord' – the same gift that the people of Israel longed to see in their king, as described by the prophet Isaiah.[16] The gifts of the Spirit nurture in us delight at all that God is and does, a delight of which, like a first love, we never grow tired.

These gifts are given that we may at last become complete and whole in Christ and know nothing less than the energy of God coursing through our veins. The writer of the letter to the church at Ephesus put it this way:

I pray that you may have the power to comprehend, with all the saints, what is the breadth and length and height and depth, and to know the love of Christ that surpasses all knowledge, so that you may be filled with all the fullness of God.[17]

This prayer is for the whole community of faith, not just the individual. This is why we need each other in the body of Christ. Slowly and imperceptibly, 'true godliness' rubs off on us as together we learn the ways of the kingdom of heaven. This is our school of true godliness, our fountain where we drink deep of the wisdom of God.

Notes

1 The prayer is based closely on Isa. 11.1–2 and relates also to 1 Cor. 12.4–11.
2 1 Cor. 1.26.
3 1 Cor. 1.25.
4 1 Cor. 2.16.
5 Ps. 62.1.
6 Mark 6.31.

7 Danish philosopher and theologian, 1813–55.
8 *On the Dedication to 'That Single Individual'*, note 2.
9 Luke 23.50–52.
10 Samuel Palmer, 1805–81.
11 Rachel Campbell-Johnston, *Mysterious Wisdom*, p. 70.
12 Matt. 11.15; 13.9; Mark 4.9, 23.
13 Luke 19.41–42.
14 1 Cor. 12.10.
15 Matt. 25.24–30.
16 Isa. 11.3.
17 Eph. 3.18–19.

9

CLAIMED

'Christ claims you for his own.'
Common Worship: Christian Initiation:
Holy Baptism, The Signing with the Cross

When he has found it, he lays it on his shoulders and rejoices.
And when he comes home, he calls together his friends and
neighbours, saying to them, 'Rejoice with me,
for I have found my sheep that was lost.'
Luke 15.5–6

When the president makes the sign of the cross on the forehead of the baptismal candidate, declaring 'Christ claims you for his own',[1] we know that we are found: lost and unwanted no longer.

The time we lost Rupee is still etched clearly in our family's corporate memory. Travelling back from a holiday in France, it was only when we stopped for a fast food fix at a diner on the A1 that our daughter Simone, then aged about six, discovered that Rupee was missing. Rupee was her treasured Rupert Bear cuddly toy, with red dungarees and a blue and white striped shirt, which lay beside her on her pillow every night and which, we now realized, lay somewhere on the ferry between Felixstowe and Zeebrugge.

Valiant attempts at consolation were in vain, and it was not until the next day that we could contact the lost property office and speak to a living voice. Having described the missing bear, we heard the man on the other end of the line say, 'Yes, he's sitting here on my desk right now!' Relief and gratitude flooded over us, coupled with a determination never to lose Rupee again. If the bear could have talked, he would no doubt have had plenty to say, but hopefully his crossness at being temporarily abandoned would have been overwhelmed by his relief at being found again, reclaimed from lost property, restored to his loved ones. He lives on still, 25 years later, patched and repaired.

We ourselves were once lost and apparently abandoned, but God has now reclaimed us. Through the rites of Christian Initiation we entered into relationship with God and our journey of discovery began. In our new-found relationship with God we experience the joy of being found again, and claimed as God's very own. We are admitted into a company of believers who are aware of their lostness without God, who have been through those dark days of abandonment and who never want to go there again.

Now we are found and claimed, we are safe once more, and in the security of God's love can begin to grow and to fulfil our promise. Now we can spread our wings, find our place in the household of God, and develop our own gifts and ministries for the common good.

When the time came for my wife and I to leave the United States to return home after nine years working there, it was a hard wrench, and the pain of parting from our wonderful faith community was not made any easier by having to sell our home just as the US housing market went into freefall. We eventually found a buyer, but on our very last day, sitting in a neighbour's house, with all our belongings in a container somewhere at sea, we received a phone call to say that in the final 'walk thru' a leak had been found in the basement. All bets were off.

Frantic negotiations ensued (with not one but two plumbers arriving on the doorstep within half an hour to give estimates – perhaps a world record). We only found out for sure that the deal was done as we prepared to board our plane back to England, as I shovelled quarters into a payphone in Philadelphia airport, desperately trying to hear what the realtor was saying as she drove from the final settlement meeting. We sat back on the plane with an immense sense of thankfulness, had a large G & T, and pinched ourselves all the way home to make sure everything was real.

'Do not fear, for I have redeemed you; I have called you by name, you are mine.'[2] These words from the prophet Isaiah, reassuring God's people of the promise of rescue, tell us why we now live in thankfulness. Thankfulness is the air we breathe, we the assembly of God's people, rescued and on our way home. We haven't arrived yet, but we have been found, and claimed, and all the rest will follow.

Paul, writing to the church at Philippi, reminds them that to have begun the journey home is the great thing, not to have completed it. Provided we know we belong to Christ, the completion of our journey is of no particular importance: 'Not that I have already obtained this or already reached the goal; but I press on to make it my own, because Christ Jesus has made me his own.'[3]

By God's grace, a previously aimless existence, lived out, it sometimes feels, as if we were perched unwanted on a shelf of the lost property office, has been transformed and filled with purpose. The call has come; we have been missed, and are now claimed. Rescue has come, and our worth and our value are reaffirmed: 'But we had to celebrate and rejoice, because this brother of yours was dead and has come to life; he was lost and has been found.'[4]

This knowledge that we are claimed as God's own is at the heart of our faith because it is at the heart of life. We are made deeply unhappy by feeling unloved and unwanted, as is readily seen in the people we meet who experienced abandonment in childhood – a parent who left home, or who had no time for them, who

parked them with relatives – which has remained a
hurt or a scar ever since. The common fear of abandonment is what makes being chosen so special.

Most of us will remember from school days the
process of team selection by which two captains
were appointed who then took turns in shouting out
names from the motley crew assembled in front of
them. Being Mr Non-Sporty, I was always last to be
chosen, along with a lad who was rather overweight.
Even for someone like me, who wished to remain as
invisible as possible on the field, it was something of
a thrill on the occasions I managed to come last but
one, instead of last of all.

Being claimed is more of a life-and-death matter in
some countries, where men gather in market squares
each morning in the hope of getting casual work for
the day. Being picked to work means food on the family's table that evening. As our world sinks deeper in
recession, such dreadful experiences may come closer
to home. Many young people are leaving school or
college with little prospect of being claimed or needed
for work, and they can become demoralized, and sometimes criminalized, by the experience. When applica-
tions are not even acknowledged, or a failure to make

the short-list not explained, it would seem that no one wants you, and no one cares. Not being claimed means that you are hardly a person any more.

For us as members of the community of faith, the moment of being solemnly claimed in the name of Christ at the signing of the cross in baptism is therefore of greater significance than ever. The deal is sealed, the partnership inaugurated, our work can begin. And wonderfully, given the inevitably fierce competition of the marketplace, here we are not being chosen for our special aptitude, or gifts or qualities, or because we look stronger or sturdier than anyone else, but simply because God loves us and wants us for ourselves. As Robert Runcie put it, 'God first loved us when we were unlovable.'[5] We have not been claimed because we are good, or suitable, or promising material, but because we are loved and treasured.

God's claiming of us is personal and one to one – that's why we know we are special – but it is not something we can keep to ourselves for long. Like people in love, we need others to talk to – endlessly – about our beloved. We need to share the joy, to sing the love songs with new meaning and intensity. That is why in Christian Initiation we are welcomed into the sacred community of those who know themselves to have been claimed by God, called by name: God's possession.

The finest and most powerful description of what we become once we have been called, and claimed and gathered up into God's arms, is found in the first letter of Peter. This is the foundation document of the people of God, the *Magna Carta* of the holy community that bears the name of Christ. In this passage the noble and illustrious titles accorded to God's chosen ones come tumbling out: 'You are a chosen race, a royal priesthood, a holy nation, God's own people.' God is the one 'who called you out of darkness into his marvellous light'.[6] As if that weren't enough, the author then rounds things off with a theme picked up from the prophet Hosea, declaring, 'Once you were not a people, but now you are God's people; once you had not received mercy, but now you have received mercy.'

Being claimed is all about being *known*, which is something all humanity craves, and without which we are incomplete. The wonder of our baptismal call is that we shall be known and understood by the one who calls and claims us: God himself. Paul, in his letter to the church at Corinth, reflects on the difference between this life and the full life in Christ to which we look forward: 'Now I know only in part; then I will know fully, even as I have been fully known.'[7]

Oh to be fully known, understood, appreciated, valued, cherished, loved, for who we are! In the end, that is all anyone longs for, and we, the community of the baptized, are those who know all these aspects of affirmation for ourselves, having been claimed by God. As we begin the liturgy, or as we launch into a new week, a new job or a fresh start, let's just pinch ourselves to recall just how unbelievably special we are to God. We are nothing less than the apple of God's eye,[8] God's pride and joy.

Notes

1 *Common Worship: Christian Initiation*, p. 86.
2 Isa. 43.1.
3 Phil. 3.12.
4 Luke 15.32.
5 Robert Runcie, Archbishop of Canterbury 1980–91, sermon at Coventry Cathedral, 22 September 1989.
6 1 Pet. 2.9.
7 1 Cor. 13.12.
8 Ps. 17.8.

RICH IN GRACE

'. . . pour upon you the riches of his grace.'
Common Worship: Christian Initiation: Holy Baptism

A good measure, pressed down, shaken together,
running over, will be put into your lap.
Luke 6.38

Immediately after those being baptized are clothed and signed with a cross, the president prays that they will have poured out upon them the riches of God's grace. This is one very good reason why we need to keep our fonts full of water at all times, preferably a little overfull, so that the water spills over to remind us, every time we gather for worship, of the lavish unconditional love of God.[1]

A dried-up empty font is a liturgical atrocity, and an empty font with a lid on it adds insult to injury. Such dead symbols speak of dryness and emptiness at the moment when we are gathered to celebrate what Bishop Martin Wharton has called 'the absurd generosity of God'.

Over the centuries the Christian font has tended to get smaller and smaller, the symbol more and more impoverished and shrivelled. We have grown more religious, less earthy. We get coy about water in church, daintily dipping our finger instead of diving in; wincing and ducking when sprinkled with holy water rather than joyfully exclaiming with Peter, 'Lord, not my feet only, but also my hands and my head!'[2]

Water gets everywhere, splashes you, runs down your neck in the rain, permeates every crevice and crack; and so does God's love. Wherever possible, our symbols need to be lavish and unrestrained, to help us constantly call to mind the wondrous gift of God, and how rich and blessed we are in our calling.

The rediscovery of baptism as central to our understanding of our Christian calling has led to much tinkering with old fonts and building of new ones. We have remembered what fun water can be. In constructing the baptismal font at Philadelphia, for example, the old font was brought out from a dark corner of the building and placed next to a new pool, with water flowing continually from old to new as a symbol of our regeneration in Christ. Here, at coffee hour after worship, the kids play, gleefully splashing each other; it's where girls being chatted up by boys trail their fingers in the water wistfully, where the men talk football. It's our gathering place.

The American liturgist Gordon Lathrop pleads for lavish and generous symbols in worship, indicative of the abundance of God's grace:

where people have begun to fill the basin again, perhaps enlarge it to a flowing pool, perhaps to place it near the entrance of the assembly room in its own strong place, the water may be seen as a symbol already. Before its use in the *ordo*, before the teaching and the name and the words are set next to it, before a candidate comes to be examined, stripped, anointed, illuminated and clothed beside it, the water is a symbol.[3]

'Give and it will be given to you. A good measure pressed down, shaken together, running over, will be put into your lap.'[4] The images of God's generosity pour from Luke's pen, and we need to use every image, every ritual, every remembrance in our worship that will help us live out that vision fully.

The image of the pouring out of God's grace helps us grasp the essential point that we for our part have to do nothing but stand under the shower head. We don't even have to construct the shower cubicle or connect it to the water supply; God does it all. Believe it or not, the hard part is just standing there and letting it happen.

Yet there seems nearly always 'one last thing' we have to do before we can stop, let everything go, and stand still long enough for the grace of God to fall upon us and envelop us. The very passivity of what is required, the discipline of it, goes against the grain of our constant activity.

Rowan Williams was making a similar point about passivity when he likened prayer to sunbathing: 'All you have to do is turn up. And then things change, at their own pace. You simply have to be there where the light can get at you.'[5] In the baptismal life we just have to stand where the water can get at us, and there is no better place for that than the gathering of the assembly where we stand expectantly beneath the grace of God.

Silence – not just brief moments between happenings but solid chunks of it – is an essential component of worship precisely because it provides periods of time when nothing is required of us but to wait upon God in stillness. These periods are marked by an absence of doing, or striving, and an emphasis upon emptying ourselves, that we may be filled with the presence of God. In silence we become acutely aware of what otherwise might escape our attention.

In David Guterson's book *Snow Falling on Cedars*, Ishmael watches his bereaved mother ladling soup, and is heartened by her ability to take pleasure in little things: the soup's smell, the heat of the woodstove and the shadows cast by the candle against the kitchen wall. He reflects that she stands there 'with the calm ease of one who feels there is certainly such a thing as grace'.[6]

Graciousness is a quality to be nurtured in our relations with one another, as in our worship, and we should never undervalue it, least of all in the Church. Whenever there is discord in the body of believers, and we wonder where the truth lies, look to see who is gracious, who is gentle and generous of spirit. These qualities are good indicators of authentic Christian life. Discerning where grace abounds, especially at times of tension or disagreement, will help us recognize individuals and communities in whom the Spirit dwells.

The recovery of many of the ancient Christian gestures and rituals has transformed our liturgies in recent decades, and restored a deeper graciousness to our worship. We often talk of a person's 'body language' in everyday social interaction, and have now come to recognize that posture and gesture – what we do with our bodies – are equally important when we come to worship God.

The restoration of the ancient custom of sharing a kiss of peace, for example, which at the Reformation disappeared from our liturgies for 400 years, helps us build grace-filled assemblies:

> when we offer each other a sign of *Christ's* peace, we are saying with our bodies that we hold dear the One who is our peace. We are believing with our bodies that the barriers between us have been broken down, the divisions undone, the ruptures repaired.[7]

Likewise the custom of standing to pray, with hands open and arms extended (again something restored from primitive Christian practice), helps us to remember who we are and to claim our inheritance. When the whole assembly (not just the president and assistants) gathers round the altar table to offer the Eucharistic Prayer, standing with hands raised in the same posture of prayer as the president, we see the Church come of age, and witness the recovery of what John Baldovin calls 'our baptismal dignity'.[8]

To grow into a person of grace may seem a daunting task, but the good news is that it begins with small and simple things, none of them beyond our reach.

In the little town of Livadia on the Greek island of Tilos, opposite the tiny 'supermarket', you will find throughout the summer an old widow, dressed in black from head to toe, basking in the sun and nodding at everyone who passes by. She sits there all day long, on the chair brought out of the house for her, both hands on her stick, leaning gently forward, bestowing her toothless grin on all and sundry. She has lived a long and no doubt hard life, but now her work is done. She lives and breathes contentment. I have no idea whether her name is Maria, but she is certainly full of grace.

Above all, the life of grace is shot through with a sense of wonder. We should never grow stale or dull of heart at the delight and beauty that pours in upon us from every side, if only we have grace-filled eyes to see. In Yann Martel's book *The Life of Pi*, the narrator explains the significance of Mr Kumar's bakery, which, because Mr Kumar was a person full of grace, was more sacred to him than any place of worship. 'I sometimes came out of that bakery feeling heavy with glory. I would climb onto my bicycle and pedal that glory through the air.'[9]

When we meet people truly generous in spirit, centred on God, eager to see the good in others and the hopefulness in every situation, always giving others the benefit of the doubt, we know ourselves to be in the presence of godly men and women, those 'whose hearts God has touched'.[10]

It is in such company that we realize our wealth in Christ, who embraced poverty to make us rich beyond telling. But we do not hoard our treasure. Like a bride on her wedding day flinging her posy over her shoulder, we chuck our treasure around, throwing out here, there and everywhere the good news of our wealth in Christ, eager that others may share what we so richly enjoy. Our joyous call is to make others rich in turn, for we are those who are 'poor yet making many rich'.[11]

Having gathered at the font as members of the holy assembly, and having touched the water, been made clean and given fresh hope, we come away 'heavy with glory'. Perhaps we need a cycle rack close to every font, so that we can go straight from our celebration at the waters of God's grace 'to pedal that glory through the air' and make the world a dazzlingly different place.

Notes

1 The enormous new font that graces the nave of Salisbury Cathedral and the repositioned and refurbished font at Peterborough Cathedral are excellent examples.

2 John 13.9.

3 Gordon Lathrop, *Holy Things*, Minneapolis: Augsburg Fortress, 1998, p. 95.

4 Luke 6.38.

5 Giles Fraser, *Guardian*, 28 July 2012.

6 David Guterson, *Snow Falling on Cedars*, London: Bloomsbury, 1995.

7 David Philippart, *Saving Signs, Wondrous Words*, p. 49.

8 John Baldovin, 'An Embodied Eucharistic Prayer', in J. Leonard and N. Mitchell, eds, *The Postures of the Assembly during the Eucharistic Prayer*, Chicago: Liturgy Training Publications, 1994, p. 5.

9 Yann Martel, *The Life of Pi*, Edinburgh: Canongate, 2002, p. 62.

10 1 Sam. 10.26.

11 2 Cor. 8.9; 6.9–10.

II

SEALED

'God has set his seal upon us.'
Common Worship: Christian Initiation:
Holy Baptism, The Welcome and Peace

In him you also . . . were marked with the seal
of the promised Holy Spirit.
Ephesians 1.13

When the bishop calls upon the assembly to share the peace in the rite of Confirmation, he reminds those present that they are a people upon whom God has set his seal.

These words from the liturgy take my mind back to the stick of bright red sealing wax kept in the 'odds and ends' drawer of the living-room sideboard of my boyhood home. That stick of sealing wax came in very handy for sealing envelopes which in my make-believe world contained important documents to be handed ceremoniously to a messenger about to ride off into the night on his trusty steed, or to a sea captain accepting command of a vessel bound for a voyage of discovery to the southern seas.

Even though we have since invented more straightforward ways of sealing documents (is it only bishops who still have fun pressing their rings into sealing wax?), the image of a seal attached by a ribbon to a document remains an effective symbol of authenticity or quality, whether of academic awards, housing construction, or pork sausages.

How wondrous, then, that God's seal is used to stamp you and me as authentic and true creatures remade in the pattern of Christ. The writer of the letter to the church at Ephesus, speaks to those newly incorporated into the community of faith when he says, 'you also . . . were marked with the seal of the promised Holy Spirit; this is the pledge of our redemption as God's own people'.[1]

As always, the New Testament emphasis is not so much on the individual standing alone, but the person as one of many, incorporated into the body of believers and made whole and complete through our mutual belonging and interdependence. Just as we need two people committed to each other if a marriage is to have meaning, so we need a loving and interactive assembly if the full life of faith is to be realized.

The sign of the cross at our baptism is a mark put upon us, by which we are branded and claimed by God. It is a badge of honour that we should be aware of at all times; whether or not it is visible to others, it is engraved on our hearts.

Emerging from University City station on Philadelphia's R3 commuter line one bright March morning, walking past Franklin Field and up through the Penn campus towards the cathedral, I encountered wave upon wave of students bearing their mark of baptism etched in ash on their foreheads. Fresh from their Ash Wednesday early Mass, they were on their way to breakfast and lectures and libraries. They were 'not ashamed to confess the faith of Christ crucified',[2] indeed they revelled in doing so. Later that same day a doctor from the hospital, still in his scrubs, stethoscope dangling, rushed into the cathedral at the end of our Mass to ask for ashing. The question of his 'flying the flag' on his ward rounds wasn't an issue; it just came naturally.

Mindful of the strictures contained in Matthew's Gospel about not being seen by others to be fasting,[3] we in our own faith community on that day were accustomed to erasing the ashes from each other's foreheads at the sharing of the peace, as a sign of forgiveness and reconciliation. And yet my heart was stirred by all those young students, and by that busy medic eager to be counted in, glad to bear on their person the sign of the cross, in a public display of allegiance that would be unlikely, if not unthinkable, in a British context. I felt good about belonging to a community of people who wanted to be marked, to be numbered and claimed and identified as one of God's own.

'Ours were the sins you bore, ours were the blows received', runs Anthony Sharpe's hauntingly beautiful Holy Week song,[4] and the mark of Christ, if borne faithfully, is not an emblem of war to be carried aloft with bravado, but a wound, our own little stigmata,[5] our tiny share in the pain of the world. To bear the cross meaningfully is to offer up ourselves to the worst that life can throw at us. It is a surrender, a little death. Here is the point at which there is a crack in our defence systems, a chink in our carefully polished armour, an opening in our skin, down into our very being.

For those living the baptismal life, this willingness to bear, in our own limited way, the wound of Christ, to be opened up, to bleed a little, is a spiritual quality we have to work at over a whole lifetime. The assembly of the baptized is our workshop where we learn the way of surrender, facilitating that openness of heart and mind without which communities of love and hope remain a pipe dream. True openness keeps us looking and listening, reluctant to close doors or to write off situations, and ready always to understand, to empathize, to forgive, to start again.

In the life of the assembly, open hearts and open minds are the special gift with which we can bless one another. When the time comes for change, large or small – a change in the time of a service or the wholesale reordering of our building – the only people available to really discuss (rather than dismiss) the issues are those with open minds.

While some may rush to the barricades, deaf to all appeals, shouting 'over my dead body!', those sealed with the Spirit of God will be noticeable for their willingness to listen, to explore, to sift through the pros and cons patiently and graciously. This doesn't necessarily mean that they will all agree – though in fact they will tend to – but they will be open to persuasion, genuinely seeing both sides, ready to change their minds, to be proved wrong, should events require it.

Being marked as Christ's own may bring to mind images of cattle being branded in the Wild West, or sheep on a hill farm being rounded up and daubed with a bright Day-Glo colour. Either way, the process involves some degree of pain or discomfort, and we should not be surprised if God's setting his seal upon us involves our being disconcerted, even momentarily unnerved. If we are to be marked down as the people who belong to God, there will be adjustments to be made to the way we approach life, and other people. In some areas we shall need to start all over again. Dogged independence and stubbornness of heart will have to be relinquished, and pride swallowed, if we are to allow ourselves to be held down long enough to be marked as one of God's own.

As we hand over our lives to God we shall also need to let go of things that own us rather than we owning them. 'Let go, let God' has become hackneyed with overuse, yet it still holds true. Many of our problems arise from our not letting go, our holding onto things – a hopeless plan, a bitter grudge, a refusal to recognize – which incapacitates or belittles us. We cling to the wreckage instead of climbing into the lifeboat and floating free.

Letting go is the essential first step. If we persist in being competent, go-it-alone people, in need of no one's help or counsel, we may get by at one level but never develop a strong loving trust of the God who is there in our falling. Paul, with his chequered history and his 'thorn in the flesh', knew only too well that his human weakness was the catalyst by which God's power was revealed in his life,[6] and we too must let our need show. This means less fretting about doing and achieving, even believing, and more focus on letting ourselves in our weakness simply fall into the strong arms of God.

The president of the Eucharist, giving thanks over bread and wine, will raise her arms and open her hands, recalling that Jesus 'opened wide his arms for us on the cross'.[7] This is fitting, for priests are marked men and women. But so are we, and that is why we do likewise, looking like the people we are supposed to be, gathered at the table. For all of us are marked, designated God's possession, sealed with God's spirit.

'Let no one make trouble for me', wrote Paul, 'for I carry the marks of Jesus branded on my body.'[8] So do we, in our own little way, in order that each of us may play our part in the work, astonishing though it may seem, of 'completing what is lacking in Christ's afflictions for the sake of his body, that is the church'.[9] We all carry upon ourselves, not just on Ash Wednesday but always, the mark of Christ that we may somehow participate in redeeming the world.

When the time came for the children of Israel, enslaved in Egypt, to make their bid for freedom, they were given precise instructions. Of crucial importance in the Exodus account is the marking of the Israelites to distinguish them from the rest of the population. Each household was commanded to slay a lamb and to paint the doorposts and lintels of their home with the lamb's blood. At the Passover meal that followed, they were told to eat standing, 'your loins girded, your sandals on your feet, and your staff in your hand',[10] for they needed to be ready for an epic journey.

We too are a marked people, distinguished by our faith and obedience to God, a people engaged in an epic journey. We too stand to eat as we partake in our ritual meal, showing that we are a people ready to move on in our great 'Passover' journey from death into life. God has set his seal upon us, and we are ready to go forth, bearing Christ's wounds, into the great adventure.

Notes

1 Eph. 1.13–14.
2 *Common Worship: Christian Initiation*, p. 68.
3 Matt. 6.16: 'And whenever you fast, do not look dismal, like the hypocrites, for they disfigure their faces so as to show others they are fasting.'
4 Anthony Sharpe, 'Ours were the sins you bore', *Celebration Hymnal for Everyone*, Great Wakening, Essex: McCrimmon, 1994.
5 Stigmata is the name given to the bodily marks or sensations of pain corresponding to the wounds of the crucified Christ, as evident in those rare mystics who experience a profound sense of union with Christ, most notably Francis of Assisi, 1181–1226.
6 2 Cor. 12.9.
7 'Eucharistic Prayer B', *Common Worship*.
8 Gal. 6.17.
9 Col. 1.24.
10 Exod. 12.11.

12

MADE A HOLY PEOPLE

'. . . you have made us a holy people in Jesus Christ our Lord.'
Common Worship: Christian Initiation:
Baptism and Confirmation, The Eucharistic Prayer

But you are chosen race, a royal priesthood,
a holy nation, God's own people.
1 Peter 2.9

In the preface of the Eucharistic Prayer at a baptism and confirmation the bishop gives thanks to God that the whole assembly has been made a holy people in Jesus Christ, raised up to new life, and renewed in the image of God's glory.

Being part of the Sunday liturgy every week is essential for each one of us because it is there that we learn the ways of holiness: there that the habit of prayer, the attitude of thankfulness, the humility of spirit and the eagerness to serve, and the godly instincts of the community of faith rub off on us. In the Sunday assembly we are we knocked into shape, smoothed, rounded, and honed into what God wants us to be. Like angular bits of rock thrown into a stone tumbler, we are polished and burnished and made to sparkle – living testimony to God's creative energy.

But a holy Church requires holy people. If communities of love and hope and transformation are to become reality, the only raw material God has available is bog-standard flesh and blood humanity: you and me. We are the building blocks from which the house of the Spirit of God is built.

Emerging from the rites of Christian Initiation, bravely clutching our light as we step out into the unknown, we shall need all the help we can get to stay focused on God, and to keep the light burning in the darkness.

On my walk to the paper shop each morning along the sea-front I am almost trampled to death by joggers and runners and by sports teams on their way to do PE on the beach. The keep-fit brigade forms a considerable slice of the population, dedicated and determined. We who follow the Way need a similar commitment to an equivalent training regime if we really mean business about being part of God's holy people. If so, what might our daily and weekly routine include?

Stillness. Precisely because daily life is so pressured and rushed and bombarded with constant noise, we need to be strict, even ruthless, about carving out a time of stillness each day when we wait upon God. People who know the value of stillness in their own lives will also insist on its place in worship, creating reservoirs of stillness experienced together from which we draw when alone during the week.

Scriptures. These treasured texts record humanity's yearning for God over thousands of years. Through immersing ourselves in the scriptures we are plunged into the realm where God is everything, where nothing has meaning without God. When we read the Psalms we pray the prayers that Jesus prayed; when we pore over the Gospels we attune our thoughts and desires to the mind of Christ. As we ponder the scriptures each day we are aligned more closely to the ways of God and the instincts of the Spirit.

Prayer. Silence and the scriptures are both ingredients of a time set aside each day for prayer before God in the privacy of our own room, our own space, as commended by Jesus himself.[1] This is the bedrock of our whole relationship with God, the foundation of all that follows when we take our place in the assembly. The daily office is the name given to the set prayers for morning and evening that the Church provides. We can use the daily office at home, and also join the priest and others saying it in church.

Service. Christ personifies a life laid down for others, and those who follow him are required each day to do something beyond the call of duty, beyond what is reasonably expected, for the sake of those

we encounter who may need help or encourage-
ment. Open hearts help us to recognize those around
us whose lives would be transformed, if only for a
moment, by being touched by love. Our daily routine
of stillness and prayer equips us to be ready.

As we follow the Christian Way we soon find that we
can never be self-sufficient in matters of faith, that the
more our lives are attuned to God, the more we shall
recognize our interdependency as members together
of the body of Christ. We cannot do it alone; we need
each other to be with, to respond to, to engage with,
and to receive strength from and to give strength to
in return.

We learn to give ourselves to the cellular life of the
body of Christ – the small groups, the shared meals, the
common tasks – on which the life of the whole assembly
will be built. The period between one Sunday and the
next is too long a gap if we are serious about keeping
spiritually fit and building up the body of Christ.

The priest and theologian Martyn Percy describes
universities not as factories in which heads are stuffed
with information but 'places which profoundly
shape, form and mature those who study, developing

individuals for life and the betterment of society'.[2] The Sunday assembly is our 'university of the spirit'. Here we don't just acquire information *about* God, we live God's life in order to become different kinds of people.

In the Sunday assembly everything we have discovered in our personal search for God is brought to the table and shared. Here all that is good is nurtured and sustained, where curiosity is encouraged and where the search for the deepest meaning of all that we see and hear and that happens to us is fostered. This is where we learn to stay curious, and fascinated and full of wonder.

'You once told me', says Owen Dunne in Chad Harbach's novel *The Art of Fielding*, 'that a soul isn't something a person is born with, but something that must be built, by effort and error, study and love.'[3] So it is with our life together in Christ; it requires hard work, dedication, and abundant love.

In this process of growth into maturity and fulfilment, the prime activity that shapes us and informs our thinking and being is worship. The liturgy is indeed the holy work of the people of God (in Greek *litourgia*, 'the work of the people'), and in the doing of it we ourselves are made holy. No specialist knowledge is required, just bags of enthusiasm as we throw ourselves into it with all the gifts and talents at our disposal. As Oscar Wilde said of piano-playing, 'I don't play accurately – anyone can play accurately – but I play with wonderful expression.'[4]

Our part is to simply show up, give it all we've got, and allow God to do the rest. But how exactly does the Sunday liturgy help transform us? How does it *work*?

First, it recalls us to reality. Western society tends to dismiss the way of faith as make-believe, whereas the reverse is true; in the face of political spin, advertising hype and celebrity culture, faith recalls us to the eternal unchanging verities. We begin, in the penitential rite, with a dose of reality about ourselves and the human potential to muck things up spectacularly, identified by the writer Francis Spufford as 'HPtFtU' (I'd better leave you to work it out).[5] In the penitential rite we are prompted to face up to reality, to confess our sins, and to receive an assurance of God's mercy towards us and acceptance of us. Yes, we have messed up, but in admitting that we have, and in making ourselves part of a penitent community, we are pointed beyond our mistakes and messes to God's infinite resources of love.

Second, we expose ourselves to the sacred scriptures, as they are read aloud and proclaimed and preached to us. Putting aside our service sheet, we look at the reader, listening intently, maintaining eye contact, lest one little drop of meaning should be lost. These texts are, of course, more accurately the words of those who have sought God rather than 'the word of God', who can no more be contained in a book than in a temple. But the scriptures have borne such a weight of glory for so long that we honour them as living words with the power to bring us to our knees and to change our lives.

In the first part of the Eucharist, which we call the Liturgy of the Word, the scriptures are the tool by which the Spirit of God works on us, chipping away at our pride, opening our eyes to see, our minds to understand, warming our hearts to forgive, accept and appreciate what it must be like to live in others' shoes. We are led to see the world, and humanity, for the first time, and for that reason we can affirm our faith and offer our intercessions with sharper focus.

But words are never quite enough. So, third, we find it is time for action; we need to move. In the Liturgy of the Sacrament[6] that follows, we first share the peace, as a sign of our mutual love and reconciliation, and then take our places at the altar table. At the very least we do this in spirit, but more and more often, as church interiors are reordered and rearranged, we quite literally take our place standing *around* the table.

As we offer together the ancient prayer of thanksgiving over bread and wine, we become profoundly aware of the holiness of God's people and our contribution to that holiness. Here we are, just ordinary people, standing at God's altar, offering prayer and handling holy things, sharing communion and ministering to one another. Together we become indeed 'a chosen race, a royal priesthood',[7] and in this moment we need no one to explain it to us, for it is self-evident in who we are and in what we are doing.

After communion we sit in silence to ponder the mystery, of who we are, what we have received and what we have become in this holy liturgy. We ponder also the week ahead, girding ourselves for the tasks to which God calls us and for which he equips us in our worship.

We bask in the blessing of God, knowing ourselves beloved and cherished, rich beyond measure in the company we keep. For this, as Francis Spufford reminds us, is our love-feast, in which 'our hearts are in our eyes as we look at each other . . . engaged in the impossible experiment of trying to see each other as God sees us . . . precious beyond price'.[8] Through our participation in this holy meal we see things with fresh eyes, as if for the first time.

Here, right under our noses, is that for which we have searched at the end of rainbows. 'The kingdom of God is among you', said Jesus,[9] and it is rediscovered every time we gather for worship: 'never such happiness, never such thankfulness'.[10] Here in the offering of the Eucharist by the gathered community of the baptized, irradiated by God's Spirit, all that was lost is found, all that was stale and tawdry is made new, all that was broken in us made whole. 'Here God's "Yes" embraces and acknowledges every possible "No".'[11]

For here we are changed beyond recognition into a new creation, inhabiting a new dimension of being, where we breathe the pure oxygen of God's spirit, and where, unbelievably but yes, actually, we 'are being transformed from one degree of glory into another'.[12] Wow!

Notes

1 Matt. 6.6.
2 Martyn Percy reviewing *A Theology of Higher Education* by Mike Higton, *Church Times*, 15 June 2012.
3 Chad Harbach, *The Art of Fielding*, London: Fourth Estate, 2012, p. 503.
4 Oscar Wilde, writer, 1854–1900.
5 Francis Spufford, *Unapologetic: Why, Despite Everything, Christianity Can Still Make Surprising Emotional Sense*, London: Faber and Faber, 2012, p. 28.
6 A sacrament is one of those special meeting places with God where actions speak louder than words. A sacrament uses ordinary things to communicate a truth beyond human understanding. In the case of the Eucharist, the food of daily life – bread and wine – is used to make real to us the presence of Jesus.
7 1 Pet. 2.9.
8 Francis Spufford, *Unapologetic*, p. 202.
9 Luke 17.21.

10 Ronald Blythe describing the delight of a group of people coming together for a birthday party: 'there are cries of joy as people who have not seen each other for at least a month embrace. Never such happiness, never such thankfulness.' 'Word from Wormingford', *Church Times*, 22 June 2012.

11 Timothy Radcliffe, in Keith Pecklers (ed.), *Liturgy in a Postmodern World*, London: Continuum, 2006, p. 136.

12 2 Cor. 3.18.

AFTERWORD

'. . . walk in this light all the days of your life.'
Common Worship: Christian Initiation:
Baptism and Confirmation, The Giving of a Lighted Candle

Walk while you have the light, so that the darkness
may not overtake you . . . While you have the light,
believe in the light, that you may become children of light.
John 12:35–36

'A dog is for life, not just for Christmas', the saying
goes, and baptism and confirmation are not just for
Easter, but for keeps. 'Walk in this light all the days
of your life' are the words spoken by the president
while handing a lighted candle to the newly baptized
as the baptismal liturgy ends and they begin the rest
of their lives.

We hold up our light boldly, remembering that Jesus
named us 'the light of the world',[1] but remain aware
that we cannot always carry it alone. Sometimes we
just don't have enough hands, and need the light of
others, by which to find our place, to fulfil our own

ministry, to be truly ourselves. As members of the body of Christ we learn to run the relay race of life, each taking it in turn to hold the flame aloft.

Those who run alongside us, who yearn for God and desire holiness, are fellow members of the household of faith. Together we bring our gifts and ministries to the Sunday gathering to help make it a holy place, a crucible of transformation. In turn the holy assembly will inspire and instruct, excite and transform us, sending us forth as those who have walked with God and will never be the same again.

To quote again that hymn with which we began:

I will hold the Christlight for you
in the night-time of your fear;
I will hold my hand out to you,
speak the peace you long to hear.[2]

The Indian spiritual leader Mahatma Gandhi is reputed to have said that he had the greatest admiration for Christianity; he was just waiting for the day when someone would give it a try.[3] So here is our chance.

It's over to you. Emboldened by Christ who has gone before us, let us 'walk in this light', courageously

and joyously. Let us live the baptismal life 'fantastically and ebulliently', and let us live it to the end of
our days.

Bring us, O Lord God, at our last awakening, into
the house and gate of heaven, to enter into that
gate and dwell in that house, where there shall be
no darkness nor dazzling, but one equal light; no
noise nor silence, but one equal music; no fears nor
hopes, but one equal possession; no ends nor begin-
nings but one equal eternity; in the habitations of
thy Majesty and thy Glory, world without end.

John Donne, 1572–1631[4]

Notes

1 Matt. 5.14.
2 Richard Gillard, 'Brother, sister, let me serve you', verse 3,
   Scripture in Song, 1977.
3 Mahatma Gandhi, 1869–1948.
4 John Donne, *xxvi Sermons*, 1660, 29 February 1627/28.